i am through you so i

Reflections at Age 90

Brother David Steindl-Rast
Translated by Peter Dahm Robertson

Paulist Press
New York / Mahwah, NJ

Photo/image credits: All interior photographs are from the author's collection, copyright © 2017 by David Steindl-Rast. Used with permission.

The Scripture quotations contained herein are from the New Revised Standard Version: Catholic Edition, Copyright © 1989 and 1993, by the Division of Christian Education of the National Council of the Churches of Christ in the United States of America. Used by permission. All rights reserved.

Excerpts from "Burnt Norton," "The Dry Salvages," and "Little Gidding" from *FOUR QUARTETS* by T.S. Eliot. Copyright © 1936 by Houghton Mifflin Harcourt Publishing Company in the United States and Faber and Faber Ltd in the United Kingdom. Copyright © renewed 1964 by Thomas Stearns Eliot. Copyright 1941, 1942 by T.S. Eliot; Copyright © renewed 1969, 1970 by Esme Valerie Eliot. Reprinted by permission of Houghton Mifflin Harcourt Publishing Company and Faber and Faber Ltd. All rights reserved.

Cover/title page image by Diego Ortiz Mugica (http://www.ortizmugica.com/). Used with permission.
Cover and book design by Lynn Else

First published in German as *Ich bin durch Dich so ich* © Vier-Türme GmbH, Verlag, Münsterschwarzach 2016.

Library of Congress Control Number: 2017946397

ISBN 978-0-8091-5394-7 (paperback)
ISBN 978-1-58768-765-5 (ebook)

Published by Paulist Press
997 Macarthur Boulevard
Mahwah, New Jersey 07430

www.paulistpress.com

Printed and bound in the
United States of America

CONTENTS

PREFACE

First, a disclaimer: this book contains much that is autobiographical, but it is not actually an autobiography. For each of the nine decades of my life, I have chosen a characteristic theme and written down related memories. The nine interviews then go deeper into the respective themes. I realize that such a framework has advantages and disadvantages. One of the advantages is that it excludes details that spring only from the talkativeness of an old man and only serve curiosity. One of the disadvantages is that not all themes that were important to me fit within the framework. I was especially sorry that I could not include the dialogue between science and religion in which I have repeatedly had the privilege of participating. As a Lindisfarne Fellow since the 1970s, as speaker at the Cortona weeks of the ETH Zürich and the Waldzell Meetings of the Stift Melk, and as a participant in the Mind and Life Fellows Program, I have had the opportunity of meeting important pioneers of the sciences. My life has been additionally enriched by my friendships with Joachim Bauer, Fritjof Capra, Stanislav Grof, Amory Lovins, Pier Luigi Luisi, Reinhard Nesper, Herbert Pietschmann, Rupert Sheldrake, Tania Singer, and Richard Tarnas. To all these encounters, I owe my conviction that science and religion are two inseparable attempts to orient ourselves in the inner and outer realms of this one reality. They belong together.

I also regret that I can mention the names of only a few friends throughout the text. But here I do want to express my thanks personally to those whose help made this book possible: I was able to work on it in silent isolation on the S'Alqueria estate of Stephan and Viktoria Schmidheiny; Brigitte Kwizda-Gredler was my first reader and gave empathetic advice; Joan Casey supported me by prayer and encouragement; Johannes Kaup insightfully held the interviews; Diego Ortiz Mugica added new photographs and improved those from the past; Alberto Rizzo, Julian Fraiese, and Michael Casey helped me by helping Quicksilver, my temperamental computer; Brother Linus Eibicht, OSB (publisher), Marlene Fritsch (lector), and Rose Hofmann (rights manager) of Vier-Türme-Verlag awaited, shepherded, and published the German edition with great patience. Special thanks also to Marc Grossman for editorial advice, to Peter Dahm Robertson for translating this revised version into English, and to Father Mark-David and his team at Paulist Press for publishing it. The prayers of many friends and the encounters with many people whom I will never know by name encouraged me and strengthened me in my writing, finally bringing the book into the hands of you, the reader, to whom I am also grateful for your interest.

I want to dedicate this book to my brothers—my two biological brothers, Hans and Max, and their entire families, as well as my Brothers, the Benedictine monks of Mount Saviour, New Camaldoli, and the Gut Aich monastery at St. Gilgen; there especially, Father Johannes Pausch: this book was his idea, and I would never have written it, except in loving obedience to him as Prior.

—Brother David Steindl-Rast, OSB
Mount Saviour Monastery,
August 6, 2016

INTERVIEWER'S ACKNOWLEDGMENT

This book has an unusual style. It is divided into nine decades that sketch out the processes of learning and maturing in Brother David's life. The memories of each decade, written by Brother David himself, precede the nine interviews ("dialogues"). These dialogues attempt to explore his life and thinking as well as open new horizons of questions building on his reminiscences. Through the reflective writing, on the one hand, and the deliberate but also lively and spontaneous dialogue, on the other, two different narrative forms have emerged. There may be a tension between these two stylistic approaches, but this tension is also an aspect of the author's multifaceted person and work. Maintaining this tension, allows us in the present to take a critical and self-reflective view of Brother David's concerns with past and future.

"i am through you so i"—with this deep line of e.e. cummings, David Steindl-Rast summarizes his ninety years of life. With its many layers, this "through you"—with you, in you, because of you—reaches from birth to death and beyond; it grows accessible as he tells of his life. It can get under one's skin and touch one's heart—at least, that was my experience when I first visited Brother David in the mid-nineties in the southwest United States, and had the honor of speaking to him face-to-face. Then as now, we were separated in age by forty years, but during an encounter with him, that becomes as irrelevant as so much else. He is concerned with the Now, which transcends the flowing passage of time, bringing present, past, and future together in all their fullness.

Brother David adamantly refuses to be set on the pedestal of the master. But he remains unquestionably a spiritual master, though he has never founded or wanted to found a school. He has students all over the world, and they have not so much learned a specific method from him than they have been inspired and fascinated by his heart's wisdom, which comes out of the genuine monastic tradition, by his attitude of listening deeper and looking farther, and by the gratitude that arises from these. Anyone looking for the esoteric in Brother David—a gnostic secret knowledge that is imparted only to the wise and enlightened—will be quickly disappointed. No, for him everything begins with creation itself, with everyday reality, which can trigger in his mind questions about the meaning of our very existence. For that reason, doing the dishes—his regular chore in the monastery—is no less a spiritual activity than a theological meditation on the Holy Trinity.

Brother David is convinced that life confronts every human being with Mystery. Everyone, no matter their origins, education, culture, or religion, has an inkling of the Mystery, even if they never bother to open the doors to access it, or find them closed in their face by some religious tradition. Steindl-Rast is concerned with getting the wellsprings of faith to flow again, to make its power fruitful for shaping life, and to work toward greater justice in the world, firmly and spiritually grounded in the Mystery.

Even in his ninety-first year of life, one can still see how Brother David, who has already discovered so much, returns to being a searching novice. His beginner's mind, his multifaceted curiosity, and his sheer childlike joy attract many. He is also a living example that one can be old in years without losing any of one's mental freshness. It is possible that this is made easier when one does not need to "make" oneself but can receive one's life anew every day: "i am through you so i."

Interviewer's Acknowledgment

Thanks for this book is due to many people, not least Brother David himself; Brother Linus Eibicht, OSB, the publisher of the Vier-Türme-Verlag for initiating the project; and Prior Johannes Pausch, OSB, for his patient and persistent help in the production of the book. Additional heartfelt thanks go to Marlene Fritsch and Brigitte Kwizda-Gredler. Both spent long nights proofreading the text versions of our dialogues with watchful eyes, and giving advice along the way. Silvia Tschugg contributed constructive criticism and practical help with formatting. We are grateful to Argentinian photographer Diego Ortiz Mugica for some of the finest pictures. Most of all, I want to thank the monks of the Gut Aich monastery. They continually received me with open arms and hearts when I arrived for the dialogues in this book. Without them, this book could not have become what it is today, and what it will hopefully remain for a lengthy line of readers: a document of reflections on gratitude and of grateful living.

—Johannes Kaup
Vienna, September 1, 2016

1

BECOMING HUMAN

FINDING MY HEART'S CENTER

1926–1936

Adam in the Garden of Eden—this memory, gilded with myth, of the beginnings of human history is mirrored in what is probably my earliest memory: I am still small enough to look up at the underside of a tall tulip.[1] I can see only its underside, but I want to look inside the chalice, so my father lifts me into his arms and lets me look into the flower from above. A bitter smell rises from the tulip, its interior shining darkly with soft stamens.

We are encircled by flowers; white gravel paths lead to little ponds above which ancient linden and chestnut trees stretch out their branches: my personal Garden of Eden.[2] A high wall—which for me was the quintessence of feeling protected—surrounds the rambling park of this coffeehouse my father has inherited in the suburbs of Vienna.

My parents, my two younger brothers,[3] our "Detta,"[4] and I live in one of the side wings of this little palace from the time of Empress Maria Theresa. The central wing, meanwhile, with its large ballroom and several smaller rooms, belongs to the coffeehouse.

i am through you so i

A stone spiral staircase leads up to the second floor, which I call "the old floor" because my grandmother and great-grandmother live there. The "old floor" is my favorite place. It is where my grandmother builds me a tent using a colorful tablecloth, spread over the backs of two armchairs. In that space, I experience the feeling of belonging and being protected, and it is there that my grandmother brings me snacks and drinks. Together, we marvel at the beautiful dance of dust when sunshine streams into the room between the damask curtains. We also pray together. My grandmother introduces me to the Lord's Prayer, the Angelus prayer, and soon the entire Rosary.

At this stage of my life, my mind is still equally at home in disparate realms of reality. It is shortly before Christmas and my imagination is charged with joyous anticipation. There is something glinting on the carpet in my parents' bedroom. I take up the tiny piece of gold thread between my thumb and forefinger. What can it be? (In Austria, not Santa Claus but the Christ Child brings the gifts.) "Perhaps the Christ Child has come by already and lost a hair from his locks?" my mother suggests. That is enough to send me into a sort of ecstasy. In retrospect, too, I should say, for me, that was a genuine, albeit childlike, encounter with the unfathomable Mystery with which all of us humans must engage.

On another occasion, I look up through the trees and see something like a tiny white dove in the cloudless blue sky. Wings outstretched, it glides through the air silently and leaves a trail of huge, cloudlike letters: I M I.[5] I ask Detta what this might be, and without much interest, she answers, "That's the skywriter." I shiver with a deep reverence. For years, I did not share this experience with anyone, for adults seemed suspect to me if they could be so indifferent to something so sacred: the skywriter! That must mean the Holy Spirit! (I would never have imagined that the letters were an advertisement for detergent.)

This is also the time when I dreamt of an image that—without knowing at the time—would become fundamental to my understanding of all else that happened to me in life.[6] In the dream, I am walking down the stone spiral staircase of the "old floor." Halfway along the stairs, I am met by Jesus Christ, who is walking up from the floor below. He looks just like the picture that hangs above my grandmother's bed. We move toward one another, but instead of walking past each other, we melt into one.

The myth of paradise includes the fall of man and the expulsion from the garden. I had only just entered the second grade of my Catholic elementary school on the Rosenhügel (Hill of Roses) when my parents' divorce completely changed our life. In retrospect, I can see how young they were: my mother was only eighteen when I was born. Our coffeehouse, not far from Schönbrunn Palace, was a popular location with Viennese on day trips. Hundreds of guests came on sunny weekends, and our supply of pastry was taxed to the limits; when it rained, all the expensively purchased baked goods went to waste. To this was added the depression of the early 1930s. Each week brought agitation and disappointment, an external strain that certainly contributed to the failure of my parents' marriage. From then on, my father was gone. We three boys lived with my mother in the vacation home my parents had built in Prein on the Rax in the Eastern Alps. In the alpine valleys of the time, life often resembled the Middle Ages more than the early third millennium. More has changed there in the last eight decades than in the preceding centuries. There I experienced Christianity—the amalgamation of culture and Christian tradition, the unquestioned acceptance (albeit not complete living) of Christian values.

The holy days of the Church calendar and the local traditions gave the year a fixed structure: for Advent, we children would set up the model of the manger and would open a new window of the Advent calendar each day. Then came Christmastime, with its wonders that grew more wonderful each year. The Christ Child brought the gifts on Christmas Eve, but first we had to eat my grandmother's fish soup, which we found revolting but of which she was so proud, and then came the prayers beneath the Christmas tree, which seemed to us children to drag on endlessly before we could look at our presents. St. Stephen's Day was set apart for family visits, and on the third day of Christmas, the Feast of St. John the Evangelist, we got a sip of blessed wine—a special treat for us children. New Year's Eve brought all sorts of games of divination,[7] yielding infallible predictions of what the coming year would bring—though not taken very seriously. On Epiphany, the twelfth day of Christmas, we went star singing, but our Austrian Christmas lasted until February 2, Candlemas Day, the Presentation of the Lord, when all the candles to be used that year in church and at home received a solemn blessing. After the high spirits of carnival, we received an ash cross on our foreheads on Ash Wednesday and imposed small sacrifices on ourselves during the time of Lent. Long before Palm Sunday, we would begin searching eagerly for the most beautiful pussy willow branches for our "palm bundles," and then it was Holy Week already, with all its rich traditions: the unpopular spinach soup on Maundy Thursday, our shy kissing of the cross on Good Friday, the visit to the cenotaph of Jesus, and—in those days on Holy Saturday—the celebration of Christ's Resurrection, when the bells were ringing again, after they had "flown away" and been silent since the Gloria on Maundy Thursday. The Easter eggs and Easter ham were blessed after High Mass on Easter Sunday. Now it wouldn't be long until the village put up the maypole, and May devotions with flowers and songs to the Blessed Virgin Mary were celebrated every evening throughout the month. Taking down the maypole was no less festive than the summer solstice, when we could see St. John's Fires on every mountaintop. Our name days—celebrated even more than our birthdays—also framed the progression of the year; as did the saints' days, particularly the Assumption and all other holy days related to Mary. These "holy times" were like figures in the dance of the year for us children.

There were only two classes in the Edlach elementary school: our teacher Miss Riegler (d'Riegler Fräul'n, as she was known in the local dialect) taught the first three grades, while strict Schoolmaster Straßmaier instructed the fourth through eighth grades. Before school, the girls would dance under two linden trees in the schoolyard or play jump rope and hopscotch, and we boys had our own games, such as tug-of-war. While soccer was not permitted in the schoolyard, it was our favorite game. After all, at the time, the Austrian "Wunderteam" had even beaten the English team. We listened to cup matches over the radio, and to this day, I remember the name of our hero, Sindelar, even though spectator sports never interested me again. For days on end, my brothers and I would play explorers, following the brook that flowed past our house way up into the woods, or tend the radishes, bush peas, and tomatoes we had planted in our garden beds. In winter, we were sometimes allowed to ski to school and, on the way back, could hitch ourselves to a horse-drawn sleigh, for instance, the one with which our baker delivered bread and rolls.

I became an altar boy and had to memorize prayers of the Mass in Latin. To get to the Rorate Masses in Advent, I had to trudge through the deep snow before break of dawn. Altar boys in the parish church of Prein were even allowed to tread the bellows for the organ, but the little convent chapel of the Sisters of Mercy, on the edge of the workers' settlement in Edlach, had only the harmonium on which Sister Viola would accompany the singing on Sundays. Back at home after the Sunday Mass, we would often play "mass" again. Our friend Karli Geyer was always the priest and seemed, in our eyes, to be able to repeat the sermon word-for-word. Our young chaplain, Father Franz Rudolf Kopf—fresh out of the seminary—preached well. He had a Puch motorcycle and would sometimes let me ride on the back seat up to a nearby mountain pass to watch the night sky and learn the names of the constellations. He supported my mother—who did not remarry—and remained a fatherly friend to my brothers and me throughout our later life.

Soon, my two brothers and I were allowed to participate in the star singing on Epiphany. Each of us wanted to be the Black King, so the honor was determined by chance: our mother had baked her ring—showing St. George as dragon-slayer riding his horse—into a special Epiphany cake, and the brother whose piece contained the ring would blacken his face with soot and don the most beautiful of our paper crowns. Then, draped in linen sheets and bearing our homemade star, we set out to our neighbors' houses.

It was also a tradition for us boys to bring the newly blessed Easter fire home with us from church on Holy Saturday, so that the kitchen stove could be freshly lit with its flames. We had long before made containers from empty tin cans which we would swing on strings to fan the embers of the bracket fungus we collected and used as coal. It was important to know where exactly we had to make holes in the old tin cans. Our older playmates dutifully taught us these arts, just as the games and counting-out rhymes of the schoolyard were passed on, step-by-step and word-for-word, from the older to the younger children. It was not so easy to whittle a hazel twig into a whistle that actually did whistle loudly; or, when tending the goats, to stoke the fire in such a way as to achieve the perfect temperature for roasting jacket potatoes; or—particularly tricky—to fashion a forked twig into a reliable slingshot. Zens Ferdl was especially skilled in this regard. I can still see him shooting a swallow off the telegraph wires before my very eyes. It was dead, but still warm. I felt complicit and would have cried from guilt, but boys don't cry!

Swallows' nests were too high up in the cowshed, and the nests of the redstarts high on the gables of our roof were unreachable. But in the birchwood forest behind our house, there was a bird's nest one could peer into. Only after I had given my solemn promise never to go there alone, Sommer Hansl showed me the secret place. How artfully the nest had been woven! A single egg lay in it. Despite my promise, I snuck back on my own, but not just to look; I had to touch this egg. And suddenly, the yoke was all over my fingers. To my broken promise, I added the lie that it hadn't been me. What pangs of shame and remorse! Paradise was lost to me not just through my parents' divorce—a disgrace in those days, and something that I could not speak of to anyone even late into my adult life—but through my own guilt as well.

However, near the end of the first decade of my life, I was given the gift of the experience that would give me inner strength after my loss of paradise. The childlike dreamer had become a little rascal. I was rarely ill, thank God. And if we children ever did fall ill, our beloved Herr Doktor Bittner called at our house at any hour of the day or night. He would diagnose us as soon as he walked in, simply by the smell of the sickroom, and make us healthy again. That's how easy it seemed.

I was sitting in Dr. Bittner's waiting room with my mother—I've long forgotten my ailment at the time—and was starting to get impatient. I had already thoroughly observed the leeches in their glass, and—as inconspicuously as possible—had studied the huge goiter of the woman sitting across from us. Now I began to get really impatient. Once more I was demonstrating what I had so often been reproved for: having "mercury in the butt." But this time my mother did not say that. Instead, she laid her hand on the part in my hair and said, very quietly because of the other waiting patients, "Try to do what people in Russia do: they can sit completely still for hours, just breathing in and out and holding Jesus' name in their hearts with each breath." (That was my first encounter with the Jesus Prayer. Why my mother ascribed it to the Russians, specifically, I do not know to this day; perhaps she had read the Russian classic *The Way of a Pilgrim*. At any rate, her gift for me that day was the Prayer of the Heart.) I tried out her suggestion: I closed my eyes, breathed calmly, and thought on Jesus. Everything else happened by itself: I discovered my heart as a silent inner space where I am at home with Jesus. I began to realize that I can come home to this center whenever I want. From then on, this insight gave my life an anchor I cannot lose. It is this homecoming that gives the image of melting into one with Christ—the relatively static image I know from my dream—its dynamism.

DIALOGUE

JK: Brother David, your earliest biographical recollections reveal that, even as a child, you were filled with an unquenchable curiosity, a joy in discovery. Your world was a place where you experienced deep connections, and this feeling of connectedness seems to come from your wonder in the miraculous. On the one hand, it is wonder at nature, and on the other hand, your prayers with your grandmother probably gave you an early inkling of something intangible, something larger, greater than what is immediately around us—the gold thread, for example, which you described finding just before Christmas. In retrospect, you interpret such moments as initial meetings with a Mystery beyond understanding. Additionally, all of that was embedded in a still unbroken relationship with the Christian faith. What sort of a spiritual world was it that you were born into?

DSR: In retrospect, such wonder is truly important, central even. One could say that wonder is oriented in two directions: one is amazement at and appreciation for the beautiful; the other is reflection on it. Reflecting is more than just thinking. It means opening oneself to the things that are worth wondering over. This is the sense in which for Plato philosophy begins with wonder.[8] Both orientations have been important to me throughout my life: on the one hand, admiring and praising the beautiful, and on the other hand, wondering about something mysterious that extends beyond it.

JK: That requires some sort of resonating chamber, in your family, for instance. That's why I ask, What kind of a world was it that you were born into, for it to be possible for you to interpret those moments in such a way? That isn't an inevitable attitude.

DSR: What enabled me to take that position was a feeling of being protected. It is quite astounding that my parents and my grandmother made it possible for me to feel so protected. I was born only eight years after the end of the First World War. This was not a time of security, but of total societal collapse. And yet I grew up in this little "pre-war" world—and I mean pre-World War I! The only picture in our living room showed the Emperor Francis Joseph. I belonged to that anachronistic bubble and felt protected within it. Outside the long garden wall of our park, parades and rallies passed by with screaming and commotion. I can remember that vividly.

JK: Were these parades and rallies already connected with the rise of the National Socialists?

DSR: Possibly so. I know that the Nazi movement was already starting back then. The early 1930s were almost a time of civil war. I remember how once as a child I walked out through the large gate of the park. There were flags and screaming and I scrambled back and forth, lost between all those legs. But then I was found and brought back. So, that feeling of protection is probably the most important and fundamental feeling that made it possible for me to grow up in a sense of wonder.

JK: You were four or five years old when you had this remarkable dream where you encounter Jesus on the staircase, and as you pass one another, the two of you melt into one. This amalgamation with the Holy was foundational to you and has influenced your sense of life in the following years. Even early on, Jesus seems to have been a fascinating figure for you. Looking back, how do you make sense of that?

DSR: In fact, I find that inexplicable. But I believe that all humans are oriented toward the Great Mystery. We are conscious of the fact that we stand before what we cannot grasp. For me, this expressed itself in my dream image of Jesus. Jesus and God—for me there was no real difference at the time. I believe that as a child, Jesus was my image for the entire Divine Mystery.

JK: But in your dream, you melt into one with the Divine Mystery, so with its real image, the real presence.

DSR: And that, I believe, is a lesson that this Mystery itself gave me from the beginning. I cannot imagine it to be something that a child would think up. Thinking was not even a part of it. It was a gift of life, and it has always stayed with me.

JK: How do you feel and think about this, today?

DSR: At the very end of my biographical reflections, I write of the double realm. This double realm is something I grew into very early, and it has stayed with me throughout my entire life. Furthermore, it is becoming more and more tangible. The danger was never great that a gap would open between my thinking and my feeling. On reflection, that too was a great gift. As far as I can remember, what I felt and what I thought never came into conflict.

JK: Meaning that one stimulated the other. Or to put it differently: one could hardly think without being in some way emotionally directed, but one is often just unaware of the fact. When you feel, that influences your thinking.

DSR: And if you continue this line of thought, that means that the beautiful and the good were inseparable to me. As Theodor Haecker said, "The beautiful feels itself in feeling, and the good wills itself in willing."[9] In other words, the beautiful, the good, and the true are one. The true recognizes itself in recognizing, the good wills itself in willing, and the beautiful feels itself in feeling. For me, that has always been a single thing from the beginning. I had to gradually separate it, analyze it to distinguish its parts. But sometimes it seems to me that, in many people's minds, the beautiful and the good are not one. To them, they must be brought together gradually. My development happened somewhat differently.

JK: You seem to have had parents and grandparents who encouraged your joy in discovering the world and laid the cornerstone of a confident, creative personality in you. I know several people in whom this joy for life was halted or disappointed early, or gradually poisoned. Reflecting on your early childhood, what are you most grateful to the people around you for?

DSR: For me, the most important thing seems to be a trust in life. I received this gift of trust in two ways: First, the people close to me proved themselves to be trustworthy. They were simply there for me, the small child, when I needed them—without question. My mother was not always physically present, even if I would have liked that. I remember it very well: When she put me to bed, I would say, "Stay here, stay here! Why do you have to go?" She would always answer, "I need to earn pennies." She had to work in the coffeehouse in the evenings—but she was trustworthy. And second, I was trusted, which was just as important, though different. I was sometimes astounded at what I could do without being supervised or checked on.

JK: What sorts of things?

DSR: For example, at play. Even as small children, my brothers and I were allowed to go into the woods alone for hours, walk up the creek, and explore. I think that my mother knew where we were and that we were in no danger. We felt protected because we somehow knew that she was not far away. But she gave us that trust; so we were free. Later, we would go exploring for weeks at a time, and she did not know where we were, because at the time, there was no way to call and let her know. She gave us this gift of trust anyway, confident that we would take care of each other, that we would give each other trust and prove trustworthy. Those two aspects are what I am most grateful for.

JK: As children, we feel protected and free until we have an experience of fear—fear that we may lose something familiar, fear for our own existence. I imagine that, for you, the early divorce of your parents must have been one of those breaks. In that way, the economic and political depression of the 1930s had its parallel in private unhappiness. How did you personally experience your father's departure?

DSR: My mother and younger brother were suddenly gone. I was the only one who was already in school and thus stayed in Vienna with my father, who was very kind to me and tried hard to care for me. But taking care of a child and running the business at the same time was simply too much for him. So, he sent me to the boarding school of the Christian Brothers, where I was already enrolled as a day pupil. Of course, for such a young child, as I was, a boarding school was dreadful, but I was only there for a brief time. Then my mother came one night and simply took me with her. The separation from my father did not really feel painful, but I think I may simply have suppressed that pain. I fervently prayed that my parents would get back together. I remember that very well, but I did not consciously experience any pain of separation from my father, so I probably suppressed it.

JK: In the later years of your youth, were there any situations where you wished for a father?

DSR: No, not really. In retrospect, I feel that my mother, as far as possible, also filled the father role well. I cannot remember yearning, wishing, or searching for a father. In my early youth, just after the war—I would have been around eighteen or nineteen years old—we rediscovered our father with our mother's encouragement, and from then on, had a very good relationship with him all his life. The relationship with a father that is formed throughout the years of childhood is missing in my life.

JK: But not painfully, as you say?

DSR: It was not painful at all. In contrast, when I was separated from my mother for even three days, I missed her a great deal. But I cannot remember ever missing my father as a small child. Not in the least. But, as I said, I may have unconsciously denied and repressed my feelings.

JK: Was he less present than your mother in the family system even before the divorce?

DSR: He was very present, but he was also very strict. He was a very loving father, but when I was a small child, he was very strict about things such as eating everything on your plate. His absence, therefore, may have been freeing, in a way.

JK: Your childhood during your time in the country between Schneeberg and Rax is couched in the rhythm of the seasons, the rhythm of the holidays, and traditions of the region. As an altar boy, you were connected to the local version of the Christian tradition. But then there is also that scene, reminiscent of Mark Twain, in which you refer to yourself as a rascal, with "mercury for a behind," who not only breaks a promise but then lies about it. I'm referring to the story of the bird's nest. Psychologically, that is quite easy to understand, because one wants to preserve the integrity one is projecting outward. But you felt guilty and interpreted the story as akin to the fall from grace. Seen from the outside, that feeling is no more than a peccadillo; seen from the inside, however, it is more. How did you experience guilt at the time? And were there forms of reparation?

DSR: Guilt was connected closely to the Ten Commandments: it was very clear what one was or was not allowed to do. If I did something one was not allowed to do, I felt guilty. I did not question that. The reparation was to go to confession. I felt that as unpleasant, but then again also as very freeing. I have always found it difficult to ask for forgiveness.

JK: How did you experience your guilt? What were you afraid of if you had to live with that guilt?

DSR: I had no fear of hellfire or anything similar.

JK: Psychologically speaking, could you have lived with that guilt at the time? It may have been little guilt, but you were also very conscientious.

DSR: I was always conscientious, but that was not due to ideas such as eternal damnation. From the beginning, I trusted that God is gracious; that seemed the most important fact and the reason why everything would be alright somehow. I still remember that my mother must have felt that I did not rise on my hind legs and defend myself enough. A boy who was a bit older than I was, Löschl Loisl, was a bit of a bully, and at one point, my mother saw that and said, "Go on and defend yourself!" So, I jumped at him and hit him, and he immediately had a nosebleed. That was horrible for me. I felt so sorry for him. This was an important experience for me.

JK: That you felt sorry for him or that you could defend yourself?

DSR: No, that I felt sorry for him. I did not really doubt that I could defend myself if I wanted, but I really did not want to, because I did not want to harm others. That became very clear when I actually did harm him.

JK: There is this scene in which you are becoming impatient during a doctor's visit with your mother. It resolves very unexpectedly. In this situation, you, as a fidgeter, are introduced to the Prayer of the Heart by your mother, without knowing that it has a long tradition in Eastern Christianity. In retrospect, you describe this as one of the first turning points in which your experience of melting into Christ now calls up a complementary, dynamic experience. How do you understand this dynamic experience? What was new in this religious dimension?

DSR: As I have already said, Jesus and God were simply names for the Great Mystery. The new aspect was that now, whenever I wanted, I could have access to this Mystery in my own heart. Through the Jesus Prayer, I could go to my heart center, find Jesus there, and feel protected. That is what this experience amounts to in the end. That was something new and lasting, it is true.

JK: But it is astonishing that you had this experience so early. I imagine it made complete sense to you only later, in the time when you were a monk. Was it something you felt intuitively?

DSR: I believe it made sense to me from the very beginning. Over the course of my life, I learned to understand it more deeply and practice it better. But it made sense to me immediately. It was like a sudden enlightenment.

JK: You said that this is where a dynamic impulse is added to the experience of melting into Jesus in your dream. How do you conceive of these two sides, melting and dynamic?

DSR: What is dynamic is that I myself can actively go to this place. My dream was simply an experience that stayed in my memory. I was not even aware that it influenced me. With the Jesus Prayer, something entirely new started, which is the dynamism: there is a presence of God within me that I can approach and to which I can return repeatedly.

JK: In what kinds of situations do you feel urged or drawn to pray the Jesus Prayer, to return, as you say?

DSR: Mostly, of course, whenever the outside situation becomes difficult. In this context, I remember the dramatic experiences of bombing and war and all the things that were truly externally threatening. But I find also my own anger threatening. My own short temper has gotten me into trouble again and again. Essentially, anger has been the main point of friction with my environment.

JK: Where did your anger come from?

DSR: My mother sometimes said, "Just like your father." My father was also very short-tempered. I probably inherited that.

JK: Can you remember any situations in which your temper got the better of you?

DSR: Of course! For example, we had huge oak armchairs that came from my ancestors' old home. I once picked one up and threw it on the floor, so that it split in two.

JK: Can you still remember why?

DSR: I have not the slightest idea. The smallest causes could make me angry in such a way.

JK: Which made the Jesus Prayer something saving?

DSR: Yes. It is, of course, also possible that this anger was caused by repressed pain, such as over my parents' divorce.

JK: So, things return.... One significant Catholic intellectual movement with which you came into contact early on was what was known as the liturgical movement in the 1920s, centering around the theologian and Augustinian choirmaster Pius Parsch.[10] Parsch had advocated making the Bible and the liturgy comprehensible and immediately understandable for the people. Against the initial opposition of his superiors, who continued to advocate the

Latin liturgy, Father Pius Parsch, almost forty years before the Second Vatican Council, did something then unheard of: he held congregational Masses in the church of St. Gertrud, where parts of the Tridentine Mass were sung by the congregation in German. That won recognition at the Katholikentag in 1933, where a so-called *Singmesse* was first held. What is astonishing is that, at the age of seven, you participated at that very gathering in Vienna, holding your grandmother's hand. How much of that can you remember?

DSR: The only thing I can remember is the microphone, because my grandmother pointed it out to me explicitly: "Look, that's the Cardinal speaking into a microphone. That way we can all hear him much better." And this thing consisted of a large ring, with the actual microphone suspended in the middle of it on long springs. That image is very clear in my mind. Nothing else—no people, no flags, nothing. As for Pius Parsch: as adolescents during the war, we would walk on foot to St. Gertrud's to hear him preach. First, we had to walk through Kahlenbergerdorf down to Nussdorf. Then, up along the Danube all the way to Klosterneuburg. That was a wonderful long hike. And on quite a few Sundays, we walked that way to celebrate the Eucharist with Pius Parsch.

JK: Were you impressed by that at the time?

DSR: Very, but in my school, we were already celebrating the Mass turned toward the people—likely influenced, in fact, by Pius Parsch.

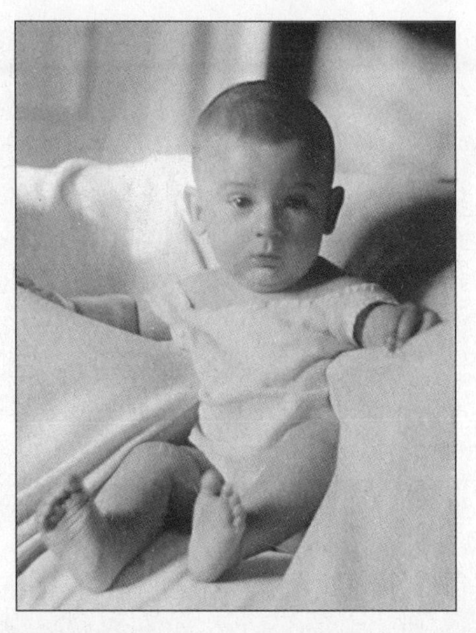

In the arms of my grandmother

2

BECOMING A CHRISTIAN

BETWEEN HUMAN DIGNITY AND HUMILIATION

1936–1946

The things we remember, but also the things we forget, say a great deal about how we see ourselves. I know that what my memory selects from my lived experience, and the structure and order I give the memories when relating them, depend on inextricably tangled connections. Nevertheless, I feel justified in singling out from the first decade of my life my dream of melting into Jesus Christ and my encounter with the Prayer of the Heart. They laid the groundwork and paved the way for my later experiences. After all, that dream was the dawn of a conception of myself that would deepen in each subsequent stage of my life—and that deepening continues today.

What seems significant about the Prayer of the Heart is that to the more static conception of who I am inside, the prayer adds the dynamic component of being able to come home into my heart. Only because I know that I can always return to my center, am I able to face what confronts me in the second decade of my life.

To begin with, there is the departure from my home, which is painful. I am sent to a secondary school, which, in my case, is a boarding school. Though the *Neulandschule*[1] gives me all that my heart, open as it is to wonder and joy, could wish for, I feel terrible homesickness when, after a weekend at home in the country, I sit on the evening train back to Vienna. Only returning to the home in the center of my heart can help me with that pain, and so I gradually learn to live in the Prayer of the Heart.

That is the only way to endure the blows that will rock my young life again and again: the Germans march into Austria and my brothers and I are suddenly *Mischlinge*, "mixed breeds." My grandmother cannot return home from America; her sister disappears in a concentration camp. Systematically, the Nazis destroy the spirit of our beloved school. I am drafted into the German army. At boot camp and in the barracks, the Jesus Prayer allows me access to a hidden inner world in which I can calmly continue to live my true life; there I am often hardly aware of the things going on "outside." Even when being bombed and during the chaos at the end of the war, I can always return to the interior of my heart, where—in the poetic words of Werner Bergengruen—"there is nothing that may frighten you; for, you are at home."[2]

Again, there are two experiences that allow me to understand my memories of these years in terms of their inner structure—two diametrically opposed experiences. The first epitomizes our lives as *Neulandschule* students and summarizes the most important things for which I am grateful to this school. Without any sanctimonious displays of pietism, the chapel service was unquestionably the heart of our school life. Even then—a lifetime before the Second Vatican Council—the altar faced the congregation. There were no chairs or pews. We stood throughout the Mass—the boys typically with their legs spread wide—or knelt on the bare floor. Much of the liturgy of the Mass was read in German and prayed by both congregation and priest. One of the prayers during the preparation of the Eucharist kept calling itself to my attention. It began with the words, "God, You created Man wonderfully in his dignity, and even more wonderfully renewed him."

Dignity was a word that I had quite possibly never encountered in everyday speech before. That might be the reason why it especially impressed me; but I slowly grew to realize that human dignity was at the core of all that mattered in our education at this school, in becoming a Christian, maybe in all of life. The very fact that we were permitted to address our teachers by their first names gave us dignity—and them as well. For "Mr. Teacher" is nothing but a title, and using a family name sounds far less personal than calling people by their given name. And, it is through personal encounters that we experience appreciation and dignity. This is what I learned at *Neulandschule*.

It would be hard to find a more harshly opposing approach to personal relationships and appreciation than in the German military. If the atmosphere of dignity at the *Neulandschule* taught me what living as a Christian means, in the barracks of the Pioneer Corps at Krems, I learned what the opposite looks like. Everything there was designed to eradicate any consciousness of human dignity. We children in uniform—for that is what we were—were trained to think of ourselves as nothing but tiny, mechanical, easily replaceable parts of the war machine. Our task was not to murder people, but quite impersonally "to kill the enemy." Self-confidence was systematically dismantled. One—in hindsight humorous—example stays with me.

As recruits, on days when we were not crawling through mud, we had to take part in classes and take oral exams in front of all others. One wrong answer and the punishment was immediately given: "Squat on your locker and scream eighty-six times: 'I am an ugly little dwarf!'" The metal lockers for our uniforms reached almost to the ceiling. Whoever had to squeeze into the space on top of them soon did feel like an ugly dwarf. The number

86, meanwhile, was the number of our Pioneer division. (Often, we wished for a lower division number.)

All the experiences in this second decade of my life can be slotted into the broad spectrum between dignity and humiliation; all have some connection to one or the other of these two opposing poles. I experienced the spirit of the *Neulandschule* for barely two years. In that time, I became acutely aware—admittedly more intuitively than by logical speculation—that being a Christian was linked to the appreciation of human dignity.

Then Hitler came. We heard on the radio how thousands in the streets cheered the invading German troops. My Jewish relatives sat weeping in the half-darkness of their apartment in the inner city of Vienna, their curtains drawn. I would never see most of them again. Soon, the shop windows of Jewish businesses lay shattered. Those who refused to participate in the boycott were denounced publicly: “This Aryan swine buys from Jews!” My mother was considered only a “half-Jew,” and therefore did not have to wear a yellow star. But during a crowded Sunday Mass, I happened to stand near a woman who was wearing one. Soon, I could hear voices: “You there, get out! There’s no room in here for Jews!” She hesitated for a moment; then she was gone. I wanted to run after her, say something comforting, but what? And already I had missed my chance. To this day, I am ashamed of that.

Hitler’s reign in Austria coincided precisely with my teenage years, so my typically teenage rebellion against authority found its obvious release in resistance to Nazi propaganda. But my rebellion was also clearly articulated in the ideal of being a Christian. We would probably have simply said, “Our Führer is Jesus Christ.” Admittedly, one could not say any such thing aloud if one valued one’s life, but we sang, “When all become disloyal, we shall remain true,” and knew secretly what we meant by those words.

We also sang the German folksong, “*Die Gedanken sind frei*” (Thoughts are free) with fervor.[3] Many of our friends from the *Neulandschule* sang that song as loudly as they could when they were arrested and taken away in police vans after attending a concert of the Don Cossack Choir. The Secret Police knew that "resistant" youths would sing Russian songs in protest and always attended the choir's concerts in droves. After one of those concerts, conducted by Serge Jaroff in September 1940, my brothers and I were fortunate to escape. Approximately two hundred others, among them our friends Bernhard and Georg von Stillfried, were held for two days by the Gestapo at their Vienna headquarters and interrogated before being given an official warning and then released. Over a dozen of those arrested that evening, however, were never seen again.

Contempt for human dignity found its most gruesome form in the slaughter of youths on the front lines. Again and again, the youth Masses we celebrated, half illegally, with Father Arnold Dolezal had to be Masses for the dead to honor recently fallen friends. And how passionate friendships are when one is so young! But time and again, a friend would be drafted into the military and be dead soon thereafter. No one could escape military service.

Then I was called up myself. My drafting orders on May 31, 1944, felt like a death sentence. I could not know that, as if by a miracle, I was to spend eight months in the barracks instead of being posted to the front, and then, at the end, be able to go into hiding at home in Vienna. Even during those dark days in the barracks, a light of humanity kept shining through in my memory, brilliant and unforgettable: Once again, as the rest of my division was sent to the front, I stayed behind because I had been assigned to a different unit. That entire unit came from the same area: they were Black Sea Germans, whose ancestors had emigrated down the Danube in the eighteenth century. These young men spoke German as one might have heard it in Vienna over a hundred years earlier. Hitler had "repatriated" them, put their wives and children in a camp somewhere, and drafted the men into the army. The dignity of these people, the regard with which they treated one another, will always remain in my memory. With what tenderness, almost shyness, they spoke of their women and children when the lights had been turned off in the sleeping hall, and with what deep sadness! After the weeks of our training together, they were sent to the front, while I, once again for some mysterious reason, was kept back at the barracks. Rumor had it that their transport train mistakenly drove into a train station occupied by Russian forces. As Russian citizens, they were considered traitors and shot on sight.

The end of the war in a city destroyed by bombs, lacking water and electricity, and without food was, admittedly, even more chaotic than the years of the war. For hours, we stood with our pails, lining up to use one or another of the few water wells that still existed in the neighborhood. Our main source of food was ragweed, a common flowering plant, that had sprung up on the rubble of bombed houses.

But amid this chaos, our chaplain, Father Alois Geiger, gave a shining sign of human dignity. Each day, punctual to the minute, he would climb over the mounds of rubble from destroyed homes to visit the survivors and offer us holy communion. Even with many of the Russian soldiers we experienced warm human relationships, especially the first wave of occupying troops that consisted of friendly young men who supplied us with bread and soup, and there were even some among them who spoke German. One of them had a wounded hand, and my mother made him a dressing with her "miracle ointment." He came back to our home every day to get the bandage replaced. One day, he was thoroughly drunk, and while bandaging his hand, my mother appealed earnestly to his conscience. The next day he refused to come into the house, but called from the street and stuck his hand through the garden gate for the bandage to be changed.

The second wave of occupation forces turned out to be far less friendly. Day and night, one could hear women yelling for help. Many were raped. Several times, my mother escaped as if by a miracle, and later fled to a convent in a different part of Vienna. The Russian soldiers were also after a Ukrainian forced laborer, Nadja, who had worked in the house across the street from ours, but had flown from the soldiers. They threatened to shoot me if I did not "send Nadja out" immediately. Our neighbor, who had heard the threat, tried to help. They let me go and shot him instead. "No one has greater love than this, to lay down one's life for one's friends" (John 15:13). I am conscious every day of the fact that I owe Viktor Springer my life.

In early summer of 1945, amid all this turmoil, the word began to spread that Vienna's Archbishop, Cardinal Innitzer, was calling on students to help the Sudeten German refugees who, exiled from newly founded Czechoslovakia, were streaming across the Austrian border by the thousands. We dressed in priest's cassocks, because that granted us at least some respect from the Russian soldiers, and set out without the slightest training, instructions, or medication. Compassion and awe for the suffering of the refugees were all we brought with us. All we could do was set up improvised camps in parish rectories and empty schools and try to ensure the greatest possible hygiene in toilets and the water supply. Here, too, regard and appreciation of their dignity amid their misery proved to be the most important, perhaps the only things we could give these poor people. Today, in the face of new waves of refugees in Austria, this memory again seems relevant.

At the end of the second decade of my life, the image of the tulip from my childhood memory reappears. This time it was in the form of ten thousand tulips that Wilhelmina, queen of the Netherlands, gave to the city of Vienna as a gift at the war's end. In April 1946, they bloomed in their springtime splendor all over the city, even in small plots of green between the ruins, where handwritten signs—"3 Russian and 5 German soldiers. Names unknown"—still marked mass graves. Nothing could have given back to humiliated people a renewed consciousness of their dignity more impressively than this truly royal gift.

DIALOGUE

JK: According to the Greek philosopher Parmenides, faith begins as a deep trust in being. To me, your years of youth seem to have been accompanied by this deep trust, which then takes shape in a specific religious practice. As an adolescent, you learned how to be a Christian, or rather, how to become Christ-like, as you have said. Your school years fell directly in the era of a fresh start in Catholicism, the Neuland movement. You attended the *Neulandschule* in Grinzing in Vienna, founded in 1926. The late 1930s, in which the German Anschluss of Austria also took place, was a humiliating time, a time that deprived people of their dignity. Meanwhile, human dignity that grew out of a Christian spirit was the lived spiritual environment at the *Neulandschule*. How did that place influence you at the time?

DSR: When I think back, the most important and decisive gift the *Neulandschule* gave me was the joy of life, expressed in a completely new way as a kind of independence. That probably also includes being personally appreciated in dignity. As students, we were taken seriously, we felt honored. Today, when I pray the verse *spiritu principalis confirma me* from Psalm 51,[4] that reminds me of the spirit of a young prince, and every time that makes me think of the *Neulandschule*. In the first two years of school, that is, in the time in which the spirit of the Bund Neuland still permeated the school, I really did feel like a young prince.

JK: What effect did that have?

DSR: Joy in life and complete trust that everything would work out—and a spirit of adventure is obviously part of that as well. The phase of a young hero going out into the world was one that I experienced very clearly and at an early age, between ten and twelve. That was also the time during which we went camping, another experience of independence.

JK: Clearly, there were some teachers who understood themselves as companions for life, as mentors and promoters.

DSR: As a boarder at *Neulandschule*, many of them I can remember well, especially our housemaster, Friedl Menschhorn, whom I feared—he was quite strict—but who also inspired me. Dr. Franz Seyr, who was my German professor, also became a dear friend to me and my family. We had the good fortune that, when the Nazis invaded, he did not need to flee and could energetically continue communicating the spirit of Neuland during that time.

JK: He wasn't replaced by someone loyal to the party?

DSR: Dr. Seyr was not the director, but our homeroom teacher. He helped me again and again—politically as well. At one point, he advocated strongly for me when I was in real trouble. I had serious problems with the Nazi leadership of the school. He managed to find the least harmful formulation to put on my report card: "A positive attitude toward national socialist schooling would seem desirable." I've kept that report card. Even in this muted form, the warning was signaling great danger. But he protected me. He also helped me a great deal by introducing me to the writings of Martin Buber and Ferdinand Ebner.[5] He himself was later the editor of Ebner's collected works.

JK: Ebner was a personal-dialogical philosopher who worked as an elementary school teacher in Gablitz near Vienna, but also one of the twentieth century's most important thinkers. Unfortunately, and unjustly, he is less well known than Buber.

DSR: Several of the things that Martin Buber was to write in *I and Thou*, Ferdinand Ebner had already published two years earlier in *The Word and the Spiritual Realities*. Throughout his entire life, Buber felt somewhat defensive in this respect. He knew that Ebner had published certain insights almost verbatim, a little earlier than Buber himself had.

JK: Did the two know each other personally?

DSR: I do not believe so.

JK: At the time, life under Nazi rule meant that people had to show their colors. You and your friends from the *Neulandschule* lived in spiritual resistance against the Gröfaz, the "greatest general of all time."[6] When you say that your counterimage was Christ as Führer, you are referring to a spiritual leader who himself can do nothing against the power and violence and terror of Nazi rule. At the same time, he must have been a powerful source of motivation for the resistance. How did faith help you at the time, in the face of brutalization, persecution, and violence? What enabled you to stay upright and even advocate for others?

DSR: The poems of Reinhold Schneider helped us a great deal.[7] We often sent out a newsletter to our friends in the military, and those would frequently contain poems by Reinhold Schneider, and of course a great deal of Rilke and things we had written ourselves. Our hero, our leader Jesus Christ, did not seem powerless to us at all. I can only speak for myself here, but what I pictured was that at some point, all this terror will be over and Christ reigns eternal.

JK: At the same time, one did see that the powers of this world were almost omnipresent and that to many, resistance against them seemed almost hopeless. Early on, what one believed in probably had little power against the things happening politically, on the battlefields, or in the concentration camps.

DSR: We did not think in those terms. There was no question that the power belonged to God and to Christ. We never doubted that. However powerful the others might play themselves up to be, it might be a difficult and very unpleasant situation, but it always remained on a completely different, much lower level.

JK: This situation was not merely unpleasant, but deadly at times.

DSR: It was a dreadful reality, but we could laugh about it. There was this joke: "The first volume is called *My Struggle*; what will the second one be called?...*My Paintings of the Island*," which implies sending Hitler, the former painter, to an island like Napoleon before him. The comparison between Napoleon and Hitler seemed appropriate. We thought that it won't be long, and he'll be gone again. That was how one thought of it, even early on. Horror and comedy need to be seen alongside each other. On the one hand, the comedy: from the very beginning, we were constantly making fun of the Eternal Reich, the Thousand-Year Reich. That it could be both ridiculous and deadly, deadly in the full sense of the word, for more of my friends than survived it—as it might have been for me by a hair's breadth—these two things somehow stand close together.

JK: Adolf Hitler, the great demagogue and nation seducer of the twentieth century, privately admired, as Friedrich Heer has shown, the historical power of the Catholic Church.[8] Though he had contempt for the Church and for clerics, and subjected them to bloody persecution, *My Struggle* actually contains a theological justification for his project of destruction, the Holocaust, when he says, "Thus did I now believe that I must act in the sense of the Almighty Creator: by defending myself against the Jews I am doing the Lord's work."[9] Hitler was not a theologian, and his thinking was certainly influenced by atheism, but he conceived of and legitimized his political actions in theological terms. The ideas of providence and destiny are another example. Consequently, he could tap into a religious language and symbolism that his adherents at least knew from cultural memory. Looking at the party conventions in Nuremberg, one can understand how well the Nazis knew to hijack religious rituals politically and reinterpret them with the goal of making people subservient. Why, in your opinion, was it possible for so many people to succumb to this fascination, to this "political religion," as Eric Voegelin has described it?[10]

DSR: Put succinctly, they were blinded. The way I understand it, Hitler, Himmler, and all these other great evildoers were blinded. Today, we present it as if Hitler had known exactly how bad his actions were, but that he cast them in a kinder light and performed them anyway. I cannot believe that. I believe that it is closer to reality to say that he was completely blinded. He truly believed that he was acting justly, for example, by exterminating the Jews.

JK: One always acts under the impression that one is doing the right thing, *sub specie boni*.[11] But Hitler had announced his intention to destroy the Jews. The idea is presented and can be read in the book *My Struggle*.

DSR: Until the end, Hitler believed that he was doing something good by doing what he did. There is something tragic in this belief; it shows the dangers of ideology and answers also why so many people fell for it. They were equally confused and let themselves be blinded by ideology.

JK: It is possible, perhaps, to explain confusion and blindness. But the question then becomes whether I start killing other human beings in the name of blindness and confusion.

DSR: That is precisely what the confusion consists of: to believe that one can feel compelled to commit injustices against others because it is God's will or the "right thing" to do. Unfortunately, that compulsion still exists today.

JK: The danger isn't over?

DSR: While we exclude *anyone* from the circle of belonging, we are "sinning." In other words, we are making a tear in the fabric of the world and of humanity. We are tearing it asunder. (*Sin* and *asunder* are related words.) Only when our sense of belonging is all-embracing can we speak of love, the lived “yes” to mutual belonging. It does not need to be the emotion of liking someone. Today, that is becoming relevant again regarding the question of refugees.

JK: Where specifically do you see that relevance?

DSR: In the question, Do we belong together, or Are those people “the others”? Are they our sisters and brothers or “a problem” to be handled somehow?

JK: Today, though, people who are afraid ask themselves certain questions. Some might think that maybe we do belong together on some higher level, but there are still too many in my immediate surroundings who do not.

DSR: In practice, of course, those are very difficult questions. But if you truly say, “We belong together on a higher level,” we need to ask ourselves how we, together, can find a solution to our problems on the lower level. How will we manage that? The point is not that others are a problem for us. No, we all *share* a problem. How can we solve it together? Our starting point must be the perspective of togetherness.

JK: Let’s return to the topic of National Socialism, to the fascination that emanated from Hitler and his movement of a fresh start. Was there tense discussion within your extended family?

DSR: There were no differences of opinion about it. Hitler was our enemy. There was no question about this at the time. But, of course, that was also caused by the fact that many members of our family were Jewish. My brothers and I were considered “quarter-Jews” as well. We did not talk about it much, but we were aware of the danger we were in.

JK: That description is based on the Nuremberg Laws regarding race. Did you feel Jewish in any sense based on cultural or religious belonging?

DSR: No, but we were close to our Jewish relatives who had to flee. My favorite aunt, my grandmother's sister, died in Auschwitz.

JK: So, to return to the topic, there were no discussions in your extended family that...

DSR: ...that there might be something good about Nazi ideology?

JK: Or that some would have taken that position out of opportunism, as was the case in some families. Some might have said, "Well, then we'll just need to come to some arrangement," or, "It's not so bad, let's wait and see," or, "Finally we can get work," or whatever other arguments were brought forward.

DSR: No, there was nothing like that in the part of my family that I knew. After the divorce, we stayed with my mother's family, and there was no debate about that, if only because my mother was a "half-Jew."

JK: If your mother, according to the Nuremberg Laws, was half-Jewish and her sisters and close relatives were deported to extermination camps, then would your greatest fear not have been for your mother? And, vice versa, did your mother not have the greater fear for you and your brothers, since as spiritual resisters, you were always in danger of being detected and persecuted by the Nazis?

DSR: It is one thing to recognize the danger and another to feel anxiety in daily life. I would call what we felt caution rather than anxiety. We just had to be cautious. One knew whom one could trust, and we even knew spies who had infiltrated the youth movement. Someone had shown us pictures of them and warned us. I can still remember it clearly. Near the end of the Number 38 tramline,[12] a friend pointed out to me a man who had tried again and again to infiltrate the movement. We were careful, but I cannot say that we lived in constant anxiety or fear. Instead, we lived in the conviction that the situation is terrible but would pass. At one point, my mother was sick in bed, and a Gestapo officer came and asked her with whom her children fraternized. She was prepared and mentioned people who really were our friends, such as Klaus and Lopi Brehm, the children of the writer Bruno Brehm, who was popular with the Nazis.[13] Because my mother looked Aryan, the Gestapo officer believed that she was the Aryan partner in her marriage. He even said to her, "It is a real shame that you married a Jew. That is just like crossing a thoroughbred horse with an ass." Afterward, all my mother said was, "If I had not been so ill, I would have jumped out of bed and strangled him."

JK: She seems to have been a brave woman, your mother.

DSR: We called her the lion mother. In the last days of the war, when the German soldiers were fleeing from the Russians, the front lines were passing through our house. One night, two wounded German soldiers came into our house and asked, "Aren't there any men here who could lead us to the German lines?" My mother was keeping a friend and me hidden; so, to get the soldiers out of the house quickly, she said, "There are no men here, but I will lead you!" Then, in her bathrobe and in the middle of the night, she led the two soldiers through the vineyards to the German troops. Then, she had to run back quickly to be home again before the Russians came after the Germans. She was also a serious mountain climber and had already been up the Matterhorn. At the time, it was not yet the tourist attraction it is today. We boys would look up cliff faces and say, "Look, Mother has been up there." We would never have dared to attempt those difficult climbs, not even later as young adults.

JK: At the time, the Catholic Church was certainly under immense pressure, even if, from today's point of view, one would have wished for more courage for resistance. How did you experience that time in which minds differed so radically, in which true Christian faith had to stand its ground in the face of a racist-populist ideology of salvation?

DSR: I experienced that only in small ways, in our own situation. At the time, we asked our spiritual counselor, Father Arnold Dolezal, "Can we kill Hitler?" It was the old question of tyrannicide. His answer was, "Yes, if you can get hold of him." The chances of that were slim.

JK: This circle around Father Dolezal, the so-called Do-Circle, was an important nest of spiritual resistance and central to your religious education?

DSR: The Do-Circle gave us religious education and strengthened our resistance in those days. Dolezal himself hid one of our friends, Alfons Stummer, in a small room behind a closet in the rectory of St. John of Nepomuk in the Praterstraße for two years. Alfons was a deserter. We knew nothing of this. No one did, back then. Father Dolezal was a brave man, indeed. In fact, he was the main figure giving us strength and stability. The Do-Circle was incredibly important to us. We celebrated Masses weekly and held discussion groups. That was our real source of strength.

JK: How big was this circle?

DSR: It got smaller and smaller because more of us kept getting drafted. But there were also many girls who were part of it. I would say we were about twenty to thirty people.

JK: During these war years, Christian ideas were one prong of resistance, but you also read a great deal of Rainer Maria Rilke in your circle of friends and in the Do-Circle: *Rilke's Book of Hours* and his story "The Lay of the Love and Death of Cornet Christoph Rilke." Why this highly aestheticized literature in the face of death and destruction?

DSR: That very fact may have been considered a retreat from harsh reality. Resistance of this kind is often accused, in retrospect, for not being aggressive enough, for pulling back. We did also read Trakl: "Mankind Marched Up before Fiery Jaws,"[14] I remember it well. But what somehow did give us stability and comfort was *Rilke's Book of Hours*. The story of the Cornet we inherited from the youth movement; it belonged to the Hitler Youth as much as to us. The youth movement only split in the mid-1930s, although slowly. One group placed the religious aspects more in the center; Neuland was part of that. The others were gradually subsumed by the Hitler Youth, but our roots were the same. It is not fashionable to say that these days, but it is true: even the Hitler Youth still promoted a good many positive values.

JK: Such as?

DSR: Such as connectedness with nature, the genuine joy in what is natural. My friends and I would not have wasted a second look at a girl who smoked, wore high heels, or put on lipstick and makeup. Our ideal was the simple life. Wiechert's *The Simple Life* was a book that both we and the young Nazis devoured in those days.[15] I do not believe that the Nazis promoted it as a decoy for less praiseworthy aims, and still, it might lure young people into the wrong camp. Those who were lured into Nazi ideology looked primarily at the positive values but came to accept all the rest. Those who could resist the lure appreciated the same positive aspects but did not accept the negative ones. That was the difference.

JK: To return to Rilke, what was fascinating, what gave strength in these days of depression? What was so fascinating for you about the *Book of Hours*?

DSR: These poems were really prayers—but written in a language that appealed greatly to us. They were so completely different from the liturgical prayers, and we could make them our own more easily. Praying was of vital importance to us in those days. One of Reinhold Schneider's poems begins with these words: "Only the praying may yet succeed in staying the sword above our heads." We'd recognize this as a thought that could give us guidance. Georg Thurmair was important to us as well.[16] The picture calendars that were popular with us often featured verses by him as captions to the pictures.

JK: In an earlier conversation, you described the war years in which so many of your friends and companions lost their lives due to bomb strikes in Vienna as "years of the utmost aliveness." How should that be understood, given the fact that you could have despaired and fallen into resignation at each stroke of fate? Where did the defiant sense of life and life-affirming courage come from?

DSR: I think that many people today experience the same thing when they encounter mortal dangers: aliveness flares up even more. For me, the reason seems to be that one is forced to live completely in the present. The degree of our aliveness is measured in the degree to which we do not cling to the past or look to the future but are truly in the *Now*. In those years, we were forced to do that, and that is why we were so alive and joyful, despite everything else.

JK: Because you were looking death in the face?

DSR: Yes, death was constantly before our eyes; so, we were forced to fully enjoy those possibly last moments of our lives.

JK: So, live each day as if it were your last.

DSR: In that sense, yes.

JK: You do not know whether you will wake up tomorrow.

DSR: As children, we had to go to the air-raid shelter practically every night during the war years.

JK: During one of those raids, you almost did not make it into the shelter.

DSR: That was at home in Vienna. Our landlord had built a private air-raid shelter in our house for his four children, and we could flee there as well. One time, we were unable to close the heavy door behind us because the air suction from falling bombs was so strong it kept pulling it back open. At that time, we had been trained to lay out our clothes in a pattern, when taking them off in the evenings, so that we would be able to find and put them on quickly even in the dark; one was not allowed to turn on the lights. A blackout was in force in Vienna. During air raids at night, we would have to dress quickly in the dark and rush to the shelter. To this day, when I take off my clothes, I arrange them in a pattern that allows me to find them in the dark. It has become a habit.

JK: After the end of the war, the Russian occupation followed, which you have described as ambivalent in that the first wave of occupying soldiers was liberating, while the second was more oppressive. As we know today, there were systematic rapes of tens of thousands of women by occupying forces. I was very touched by the scene in which you described wanting to protect Nadja, a Ukrainian forced laborer from your neighborhood, and how a neighbor came to your aid. This neighbor paid for his moral courage with his life. Did you feel at the time that your last hour had come—or rather, that by an act of providence you had escaped with your life?

DSR: I was in a state of complete shock. I did not even think of that aspect. But I should clarify, we were not hiding Nadja. We simply did not know where she was. She had gone. She simply fled. One could not say that I was not afraid; I was simply in shock.

JK: Then why was your neighbor shot?

DSR: The Russian soldiers were probably drunk. They wanted to find this girl and could not, so they threatened to shoot someone if she did not appear. They let us go because they were distracted by Mr. Springer; now he caught their attention. But he was not the only one. They rounded up some ten or twenty people, marched them to the church, and stood them up against a wall. The soldiers shot wildly in the air, but in the end, Mr. Springer was dead. They may not have intended that at all. No others were hurt. Viktor Springer lived in the house next to ours, and the Springers had a forced laborer too, an older woman from Poland, named Sophie. She saw me in uniform many times, but when the Russians asked her, "Is he not a soldier as well?" she said, "No, no, he's just a child." By doing that, she saved my life.

JK: As did Viktor Springer.

DSR: Yes. I think of him as having saved my life. When the soldiers were menacing us in the other house, he came to the garden gate and shook it. They heard the noise, let us go, ran down, and shot him.

JK: So, to clarify the situation, the two Russian soldiers were looking for Nadja but came into your house and questioned you, if one can call it that.

DSR: I suppose I must have been standing somewhere close by. It all happened in the street, in this broad suburban road with no traffic. Then the soldiers led me not into the house in which we lived but to the second floor of a villa on the opposite side of the street where a resistance fighter who had been an officer in the First World War lived. He was probably too old to be drafted by then.

He was active in the resistance and very brave. In this moment, he kept talking to the soldiers who had put their machine guns to our heads. His wife was standing there as well. They had put a bucket over her head. He kept talking to the Russians—in German—and I suppose it is difficult to shoot at someone who keeps talking to you. Soon, Viktor Springer was rattling the gate downstairs. So, they turned, left us standing there, and we were spared.

JK: That saved your life. In all the turmoil after the end of the war, with millions of refugees, you and your friends followed Cardinal Innitzer's call to assist the Sudeten-German refugees.[17] You write that you had no specific training and no knowledge: "Compassion and awe for the suffering of the refugees were all we brought with us." What reaction did these actions cause in you?

DSR: It was yet another kind of encounter with great human suffering.

JK: Some of the Sudeten-Germans even came on foot.

DSR: All of them came on foot. Some of them pulled little carts onto which they had packed all their possessions. That was the first time I had to give practical care to truly poor people. There was hardly anything we could do. We saw to it that they were housed in relatively humane conditions and had clean water and toilets that were at least reasonably hygienic to prevent cholera and dysentery.

JK: What encounters can you recall from that experience?

DSR: I can remember children, for example, who had bloody knuckles from knocking at doors begging. Seeing that, we organized little groups to go stealing cherries. There was no one who could have harvested them anyway. One evening, several children arrived pulling a handcart and said, "Mother is lying back there on the road and having a baby." We had nothing but a bicycle, on which we went to look for her—and found her. The child had not yet come, thank God. We then led her back to the camp slowly, where she had the child.

JK: That is truly an incredibly exciting time, to swing back and forth between life and death and experience all the emotions.

DSR: It was certainly formative, but we only attended to what needed to be done, moment by moment. There was no time at all to think about it. This needs to be done, let's do it. We did not think of anything more. It never entered our minds to muse on how terrible it all was.

JK: So, you might say that it was a completely human impulse, which you were then able to see in a larger interpretive framework of faith.

DSR: It was nice that we could do this work within the framework of the Church. As Catholic youth, we were in the heart of the places where it was happening. The only help we could always count on were the priests. They made the schools available to us as dormitories for the refugees and used the pulpit to ask for things we needed. Many priests hid and even defended women from the Russians in their churches and rectories.

JK: Defended in what way?

DSR: One day, we came to a village where a pastor had hidden about forty women in the parish hall. A Russian soldier broke into the building, but the pastor grabbed him and dragged him out. He tried to drown him in a small stream, at which point the soldier bit off his thumb. So, we were greeted by a pastor with only one thumb.

JK: Did he drown him in the end?

DSR: No, the Russian soldier ran away.

JK: And never returned?

DSR: As far as I know, he was never seen again.

JK: Quite the stories...

DSR: Of course, in the end, we did all get diarrhea; many of the refugees as well, I'm sure. Following that, I had to return to Vienna. The great gift of those weeks was that we learned compassion. For me, this was the important lesson in becoming a Christian. On special occasions, an uncle brought us sausages. We all suspected strongly that they were made of dog meat, but no one said a word; we were so happy to have meat of any kind. Once, my brother Max ate around a small piece of that sausage on his plate to save it as the final climax of his meal. When only that little morsel was left, I swooped down on it with my fork and gobbled it up. This was meant as a joke, but that sixteen-year-old-young man broke into tears. My shame also taught me compassion.

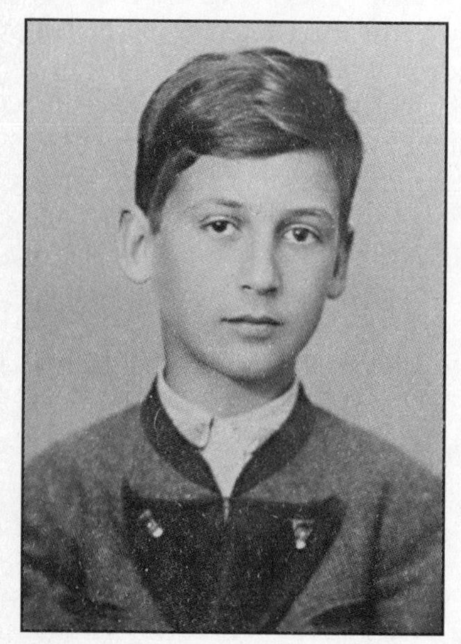

3

DECISION

1946–1956

My amazement knows no bounds—the war is over and I am still alive! It dawns on me slowly at first; then, suddenly, I can see it clearly: a whole lifetime stretches before me! I am overwhelmed, overjoyed, and at the same time, frightened by this insight—frightened because I sense that this is as great a gift as it is a responsibility. What should I now make of my life? Seizing any one of the countless opportunities before me means letting go of all the others. How should I find my priorities? Looking forward, I grapple with these questions, knowing that what I do will be less important to me than that I do it with joy. And looking back at the years of war, I see that in the darkest, most unhappy moments, an inner joy gave me strength. It was a joy that did not depend on happiness or unhappiness. But on what did it depend? I brood over this question. And then, out of the blue, a sentence pops into my mind: "To have death before one's eyes at all times." Yes, really, "out of the blue"—out of the most joyous blue sky. It is a bright August day in Salzburg. I have been invited here by friends, among them an enchanting girl on whom I have a crush. The city is filled with music; everywhere, summer breezes carry tunes across streets and squares, down promenades and through open windows. It's 1946, the first year that the Salzburg Music Festival is once again being held in a free Austria. In exchange for a packet of American cigarettes, an usher casually discovers two free orchestra seats and Elisabeth and I can hear and see Mozart's *Don Giovanni*.

The end of that opera again brings the words to my mind: "To have death before one's eyes at all times." This sentence keeps going around in my head. It comes from the Rule of St. Benedict, a short book, almost fifteen hundred years old. I had read it as a student because, to spite the authoritarian regime, we would read anything that displeased the government. These few words hit me more than all the rest of the book, and now it begins to dawn on me why: these past years, we young people have had death before our eyes, so close we could touch it. More of my friends were killed at the front lines than survived it. And at home, too, bombs had brought daily destruction and death. A single incautiously whispered word could mean one's end; one of our chaplains was arrested in church and executed.[1]

But despite all that, looking back, I must say that for my friends and me those terrible years of war were also years of true joy, a joy I wish never to lose. Hence the question, what gave us that joy? Suddenly, I can see the answer: We lived with such joy because we were forced to have death before our eyes constantly. Thus, we had to live in the moment—completely in the *Now*—and that was, in the past, the secret to our joy.

Since I do not ever want to lose this spark of joyous aliveness, in the future, too, I will need to "hold death before my eyes at all times." I had found this guiding thought in the Rule of St. Benedict. Did that mean that I would need to become a Benedictine monk? At the time, this thought made me queasy, and so I preferred to go dancing. No one dances the polka with as much fire as my Elisabeth. The two of us lived on a hill overlooking St. Peter's Archabbey, and each morning, I walked down to celebrate Mass with the Benedictine monks. In my Schott Missal, I followed along with the Latin Mass texts for the day in German. Every day, it seemed that the reading, yet again, concerned decisions. I am captivated by the topic of decision-making, even if only half consciously. Hesitantly, I consider whether that all-important joy might even be worth becoming a monk for. I am divided against myself but shrink back from making a decision. The next morning, the first reading at Mass speaks of the famous judgment of Solomon in 1 Kings 3: two women bring one child before the king, and each claims the child is hers. Solomon calls for a sword and says, "Divide the living boy in two; then give half to the one, and half to the other. One of the women cries out, "Please, my lord, give her the living boy; certainly do not kill him!" (vv. 25, 26) thus proving herself to be the true mother.[2]

In that moment, something in me cries out as well, and I've made my decision. Of course, it's perfectly illogical, but I now know that becoming a monk will be my path, however far the detours may lead me.

I will run away from the consequences of this decision for the next seven years, finding one alibi after the next: studies at the Academy of Fine Arts, a diploma as an art restorer, cofounding a successful children's magazine,[3] working as a restorer, journeying to the United States, studying anthropology, travels as prefect of the Vienna Boys' Choir, a year in Florida, a doctorate in psychology at the University of Vienna....

In truth, I had been unknowingly prepared for the experience of my "calling." After the war, my brothers and I renewed contact with our father. He was now living in East Tirol and got me a job as a farmhand over the summer holidays. Hard work and hearty farmers' meals sound seductive—but on the second day, I am sent straight up to a mountain pasture, known as the Alm. Here, food is less plentiful, but the solitude and silence, surrounded by the peaks of the Dolomite Mountains, become an experience of deep contemplation and inner joy.

The only other people up on the Kerschbaumer Alm are "Uncle" and "Aunt"—distant relatives of the farmer for whom I am working—who have lost their homes in the war. We live primarily off Sterz:[4] Aunt cooks, Uncle and I sit across from one another, and Aunt puts the pan between us. On the first evening, we both start at our edge and work our way toward the center of the pan, but Uncle is quicker and works his way past the middle into my territory. From then on, I start our meals by making a line down the middle of the pan and eating from the center toward me. That way, we get along. I learn to milk and otherwise handle sheep and young cattle. I can walk across the Alm for hours, listening to the silence and reading my pocket Bible—particularly the psalms, which I read over and over. But I also read the Song of Songs, the other Wisdom Writings, and the stories about King David, who also began his life as a shepherd.

I remember a moment from the first year after the war that casts light on the circuitous path from my beatific experience on the Alm to my similar later experience as a novice: A few friends and I are standing in a crowded tramcar. We are talking about our plans; the others seem to have clear-cut career paths in mind. Something in me resists such clarity. "I'd like to encounter many different things before I make my decision," I hear myself saying, and listen, astonished, as I spontaneously use a metaphor to express my idea: "The broader the base, the higher the pyramid."

So, to expand the "base of the pyramid," I study at the Academy of Fine Arts, where I passed the entrance exam during the war. And since I am interested in primitivism and children's art, I also study ethnology and developmental psychology at the university. Bombs have destroyed the university buildings, so the first thing we students must do is help with the reconstruction. We do so with the joy of new beginnings and rebuilding. After we have completed the mandated hours of shoveling rubble—marked in our student passes—we are permitted to enroll in a course of study.

Decision

In the summer of 1947, I visit the United States for the first time. Even the crossing on the SS Marine Falcon, a small troop transport ship, is an adventure. I have been invited to a convention of Young Christian Students in Chicago. I still remember how, one evening, our Austrian delegation was supposed to sing Austrian folk songs, but how all of us began to cry so much from homesickness that we could not keep singing. From Chicago, American students give my French friend, Isabel, and me a ride to California. From there, we return to New York by bus, which takes an entire week. Then we board a ship of the Holland American Line back to Europe. (At the time, flying across the Atlantic was financially out of the reach of mere mortals.)

My second journey to the States is initially planned as a visit to my grandmother and to my two brothers studying in New York—but a surprise extends the trip. While I am in New York, I receive a telegram from the Vienna Boys' Choir stating that one of the prefects has been denied an entry visa at the last minute. Could I accompany the Choir on their North American tour in his stead? The invitation came because I had worked as prefect of the Choir during my summer vacation, and their rector, Monsignor Joseph Schnitt, had come to know me. And so, for over three months, I get to ride on the Choir bus across the United States, including brief visits to Mexico and Canada. We give two concerts every three days and cover more than two hundred miles a day. This is very taxing for the children. I have nothing to do with their musical education, but must instead ensure their physical and mental well-being. One of the boys, Werner Scholz, will remain my lifelong friend.

One minor event on this tour with the Vienna Choir Boys was to gain major importance for me: an American choir, the Apollo Boys' Choir, invited the Viennese boys for a little party while we were in Palm Beach, Florida. On that occasion, their founder and director, Coleman Cooper, suggested to me that I might want to work as a prefect in his choir after the Vienna Boys' Choir return to Austria. The prospect of living in Florida and in Palm Beach at that, was tempting enough, but I would be living in a most beautiful palazzo, imaginatively decorated in the style of the Italian renaissance. In the early 1920s, Philadelphia art patron Joseph E. Widener had commissioned architect Maurice Fatio to create Il Palmetto. The elegantly landscaped grounds of this estate extended across the entire strip of land between Lake Worth and the Atlantic Ocean. Recently, this paradise had become the home of the Apollo Boys' Choir. Throughout my life, I have often had the privilege of calling exceptionally beautiful places home. None of them was more enchanting than Il Palmetto, where "Mama Cooper," as the boys called her, cared for them and me as a mother would. It was an additional piece of good fortune that I was allowed access to the choir's recording equipment, as I was working on my dissertation about vocal expressiveness at the time. In those days, recording devices were extremely expensive, and their operation was nowhere near as simple as it is today. The magnetic tape kept jumping off the reels, or it would tear and have to be spliced; sometimes I was entangled in tape from head to toe, like Laocoön in the serpents. When I had finally collected the necessary material, I returned to Vienna, wrote my dissertation, and attained my doctorate in psychology in November 1952 under Professor Hubert Rohrbacher. Fortunately, I was able to return to New York City that same year, in time to celebrate Christmas with my family. That winter journey across the storm-tossed Atlantic would be my last crossing on a steamship. Only many years later would I return to Europe—that time by airplane.

This, my third stay in the United States—not the sort of place one seeks out to become a monk—was soon to become a time of crisis for me. After all, this time I had not merely come for a visit, but to immigrate. True, I was happy to be with my family, but city life in Manhattan was not for me. The only place I truly felt at home was the silent reading room of the Public Library on 42nd Street. I spent countless joyful hours in the library's huge, dimly lit, high-vaulted halls, and to this day, I am grateful for the gift this was to me.

One of my older cousins was a psychiatrist in New Jersey, and he let me work for him on some cases of mentally ill children. A former colleague from the Vienna Academy of Fine Arts already had a prominent position at the Philadelphia College of Art, and I received work from him as well. But my heart was not in it, nor did I know where it belonged or where it could find rest.

My culture shock in the "New World" soon led to days of depression. I had come here to escape, but now I began to ask myself whether the right monastery might not be waiting for me somewhere after all, even in the United States. "If I had lived in the Middle Ages," I said to a friend, "I might have become a Benedictine monk, but today, too much tradition is weighing down the monasteries in Europe. What I'm looking for"—yes, I heard myself saying that I was actually looking for something!—"is a monastery that follows the original Rule." "That's strange!" my friend replied. "I hear that kind of reformed monastery has just been founded near Elmira in New York State." That same day, I called the Greyhound Bus Company, found a night bus to Elmira, arrived there the next morning, and after some searching, discovered the farm on which three monks had founded the monastic community of Mount Saviour.[5] That afternoon, I worked with one of them, Father Placid. While we were planting squash, he answered my questions and his answers reassured me. The next morning, I hitched a ride with two other guests back to New York. That was in mid-May of 1953. Suddenly, the decision had become easy. I applied at Mount Saviour, was accepted as a candidate, and on August 20, I arrived to stay.

In my first years at the monastery—as postulant, as novice, and then as a young monk—I felt quite like I had felt as a shepherd on that mountain pasture in Austria. The third decade of my life ended in the rolling hills of the Iroquois much as it had begun high in the Alps. What I had been doing there all day long, I did now: listen deeply into silent space.

DIALOGUE

JK: The art of living well is also the art of dying well—*ars vivendi est ars moriendi*. You had already read the Rule of St. Benedict during the war, and in the face of the daily possibility of death, you got to know central spiritual principles. When people speak of religion today, many think of ways of life that are controlled from outside, marked by rules and commandments. For those people, religion is problematic, irrational, a potential source of conflict. Only few associate spirituality with being alive, wakeful, and living fully. But this aliveness and all its possibilities were available to you, Brother David, in a freed Austria after the end of the war. You not only had death constantly before your eyes, but a whole bouquet of options. Which were the ones that attracted you most, initially?

DSR: At first, I wanted to continue what I had already begun before I was drafted: my studies at the Vienna Academy of Fine Arts. But Professor Karl Sterrer, whom I loved and admired greatly, had been caught in the political wheels. Even though he had been known to be opposed to Nazi ideology at the time I studied with him, he now was made a scapegoat. He was no longer allowed to teach at the Academy. I never found another painting teacher who fit me well, so I switched from painting to studying art restoring with Professor Eigenberger. That was fascinating. After the war, as restorers we received a great many damaged art objects.

JK: In what sorts of places did you do your restoring work?

DSR: With a few exceptions, we worked in the Academy's studio, for example, on a painting by Lucas Cranach, the paint of which had bubbled during a fire—I think it was the fire in St. Stephen's Cathedral. We had to use a great deal of care and effort in repairing that painting. There was also a work by Albrecht Dürer: a Madonna belonging to the Austrian state, which was then traded in, so that Austria acquired the Stifter Museum from the Czech city of Oberplan. Another thing that was very exciting for us students was that every day from noon to 1:00 p.m., the professor would offer free expertise to people who wanted a valuation of their real or supposed art treasures. We students could sit in on this every day. Most of the time the things weren't very valuable; paintings often turned out to be mere copies of masterworks. But once, someone brought in a briefcase a folded canvas, and our professor immediately said, "That could be something interesting. We need to take a closer look at it." It was impossible to see the picture clearly, since it had darkened and was extremely dirty. After weeks of work, it turned out to be a previously unknown Van Dyck. We were the first to discover it. There really were some very exciting moments at the Academy. But what excited me much more during this time was a lecture by Professor Koppers on the origins of the idea of God.[6]

JK: He was a theologian?

DSR: No, he was an anthropologist, but he was a priest of the Society of the Divine Word (SVD). At the time, they provided several professors of the anthropology department. Yes, I was very moved by this lecture. I went to the Austrian National Library afterward and borrowed the various volumes of Wilhelm Schmidt's *The Origins of the Idea of God*.[7] I sat in the Café Bastei on the Schottenring, and wept as I read. Following that, I studied anthropology.

JK: Can you remember what it was about the book that moved you to tears? Was there a special idea or realization that stirred you?

DSR: Wilhelm Schmidt's Kulturkreis theory is largely obsolete today. But what remains and what really touched me at the time was that the God Idea is a shared primeval human experience. That is what Father Wilhelm Schmidt's volumes illuminated for me.

JK: That there has always been a kind of primeval religiousness or faith with all peoples—is that what you mean?

DSR: He articulated it quite differently then, but that thought continued in my mind. Today, I can see that what makes us human is that we grapple with this Great Mystery that we can cautiously call God. This idea shone on me like a light in that moment, and that moved me so greatly.

JK: So, you studied anthropology. You describe the summer of 1946 as free and magical. If I interpret it correctly, you as a then twenty-year-old were in love with a girl named Elisabeth. You wrote that she was an excellent dancer and that you not only visited the Salzburg Festival with her but also did quite a bit of dancing yourself. If you were in love, then were you considering marrying and founding a family?

DSR: No, I did not consider it, so much as plan it. I pictured it in detail: I wanted to have twelve children. But soon, I began considering the problem of overpopulation, and eventually that consideration did decisively contribute to my decision to live a celibate life.

JK: You thought that you didn't want to bring more children into the world because there were already too many? But that was back in 1945, when the world population was only two billion people.

DSR: Since then, humanity has tripled in size. That is completely unimaginable.

JK: When you're in love, you don't necessarily think of overpopulation.

DSR: Today, young people do not even necessarily think of a family and children. But at the time, we did think of that. It was part of our frame of reference.

JK: For both of you?

DSR: In our entire generation's frame of reference, love, marriage, and family still belonged together, that is what I mean.

JK: So, you pictured it for yourself. And on Elisabeth's side?

DSR: I do not know. But I believe that picturing was rather one-sided.

JK: Your love as well?

DSR: Largely.

JK: At any rate, nothing more came of that on the relationship level. But at the time, you didn't yet know that you wanted to live alone, did you?

DSR: Since my experience at St. Peter's Archabbey in Salzburg, I did know, somewhere deep inside, that this was my path: becoming a monk.

JK: You are referring to the scene where, as part of a service in St. Peter's, you hear the Bible text on the judgment of Solomon—a child is to be split with swords, and the true mother saves the child by giving it up. You relate this text to your own life: you did not want to live feeling torn in two. But why did you relate it to yourself at all? In what ways did this wholeness take shape for you?

DSR: At that time, I had this "either/or" in my head constantly and felt the dangers of inner division. I became aware that we had always been whole, undivided. That is why we were so happy even during the war. We had to live in the moment because death was always before our eyes. I then connected the experience of "keeping death before your eyes at all times" with being a monk, because I had read the sentence in the Rule of St. Benedict. I realized that, as a monk, my life would become whole; I would live in the moment and be happy. So, I wanted to become a monk, but at the same time, I didn't want to.

JK: So, at the same time, twelve children would have been an attractive option as well, were it not for overpopulation?

DSR: Very attractive, and many other things were as well. At the time, I pictured being a monk as something quite grim. I was still undecided in this "either/or."

JK: Had you read Søren Kierkegaard at the time, his book *Either/Or*?

DSR: We did read Kierkegaard during the war, but I do not think that had any influence on my decision. It is told that, at a reception, a society lady enthusiastically thanked Kierkegaard for his book *Either* AND *Or*. I was the same way. I wanted both: either and or. But the judgment of Solomon made me reflect.

JK: So, you are saying that at age twenty, you realized that you wanted to live in wholeness. And yet for several more years you continued living that "either *and* or."

DSR: Precisely. Often in life, an insight appears long before it is finally put into practice or even before there is any will to put it into practice. I lived this "either *and* or" and was unwilling to decide, despite being simultaneously able to see that I did not want to live a divided life. I could see this particularly clearly after the Bible reading of the judgment of Solomon.

JK: Can you remember why it was particularly this passage that spoke to you and gave you such clarity?

DSR: The imagery is very clear: to me, the two women were, on the one hand, the Church, the true mother; and on the other, the world, both claiming “this child is mine!” The true mother lets go of her child to keep it alive—but in the end, the judgment of Solomon restores it to her. That image did not let go of me, even though I was constantly pushing it away from my conscious mind.

JK: ...and went on to completely different studies. The broader the base, the higher the pyramid—as you described your motivation for such varied coursework at the University of Vienna. After anthropology, there were art, restoration, and even psychology. This last course you studied with Hubert Rohracher, who was born in East Tirol but taught in Vienna.[8] From today’s point of view, you see these studies also as an attempt to escape your final decision to become a monk. I remember that you once told me how heavy another reason weighed: at the time, you felt yourself to be anticlerical, in the sense of seeing the Church as still having many very bourgeois aspects. That was the sense in which the Neuland movement was anticlerical; not antireligious and certainly pious, but anticlerical in its rejection of the old, ivory tower Catholic system.

DSR: For me, the monasteries, at least those that I knew, were largely part of that outdated system. The only monastery I felt at home in was Heiligenkreuz Abbey, where Father Walter Schücker was my spiritual counselor.[9] But because my enthusiasm had been awakened by the Rule of St. Benedict, I always longed for a monastery that followed the original Rule. That was, admittedly, what kids today would call “a head trip.”

JK: What did you hope for from this "back-to-the-roots" approach?

DSR: I do not believe I pictured anything precise. I knew more what I did not want than what I wanted. But I did not want what I had seen.

JK: Such as? What did you not want?

DSR: An abbey with so many parishes that you really become more of a parish priest than a monk by joining it. My ideal was to go back to the original monastic practice without all this historical baggage. That was what I told my friend, Father Phillip Walsh, an Oratorian in the United States. In response, he told me of a newly founded monastery that had made it their goal to live strictly by the Rule of St. Benedict. That was the first time I heard of Mount Saviour.

JK: We'll get back to that. I want to take a closer look at the time of your early twenties. You spent a relatively lengthy period in East Tirol, on the Kerschbaumer Alm, an Alpine farm, surrounded by the silence of the mountains. On reflection, you could see that time as an incubation period for your later life as a monk. On the Alm, the dividedness may have lifted. Life there is simple and clear; things like daily rhythms, the weather, the animals, the water, milk, cheese, meat, and bread. It is easier to retreat there, there is little distraction. But when you come back down into the valley with its varied ways of living, all the temptations return. And one can't live up on the mountain indefinitely. To a certain degree, that was a symbol of your dividedness or ambivalence back then, which lasted quite a while into your subsequent years.

DSR: The thing about the Alm that was so beautiful to me was the opportunity for deepening. And what was so beautiful about the valley was the possibility for broadening. Now that the war was over, we could, for the first time, travel abroad. I went to Switzerland. That was a broadening experience for me, if there ever was one. Here, everything was a discovery for me—a land of peace and plenty. Together with two friends to whom I still have a close connection—Werner Scholz, the former choirboy, and Heinz Thonhauser from Lienz—I went on a bicycle tour. We rode through East Tirol into Switzerland and to the lakes in northern Italy. It was a time full of broadening experiences. Today, it is hard to imagine what it meant to us after the war to see the world and be free and mobile enough to simply ride a bike to wherever one wanted to go. Those were significant experiences of breadth. So, that was my conflict: whether to go deep or broad.

JK: Back to the Alm: it was a "natural monastery," where you were able to experience contemplative life. Nature itself was the monastery; you even had a sort of hermit's setting in that solitude.

DSR: I would call it the experience of a reflective life. On the Alm, I experienced a time of joyous meditation—all day long. I was either filled with joy in nature or with joy in reading the small Bible that I carried with me.

JK: So, you read the book of nature and the Books of the Bible?

DSR: I did not think of it in those terms at the time, but St. Bernard of Clairvaux did say that there are these two books in which we can find God. The Book of the Holy Scriptures and the book of nature.

JK: And what you perused, so to speak, in East Tirol was the book of nature?

DSR: Yes. What could be more beautiful than a mountain pasture, completely cut off from the rest of the world? There was not a single person there aside from us all summer. Only once or twice did pilgrims come by; the border between Austria and Italy—right above the Alm—was closed at the time. All around our meadows, like a fence, stood the delicately carved peaks of the Dolomite Mountains, white against blue sky...unbelievably beautiful.

JK: Here it is again, that encounter with the wonderful as you knew it from your early childhood, when, with your father's help, you look into a tulip and are transfixed by what you find.

DSR: The entire Alm was like the chalice of a flower, with the surrounding mountain peaks as its petals, and us sitting in the center.

JK: After your second journey to the United States, you followed your family to America in 1951. Your relatives had already immigrated there and were living in Manhattan, New York. But the question of finally deciding whether to become a monk would not let you go. It is an irony of history that, in the land of possibility, you finally found your possibility, a monastery of your choice in Elmira, where the Benedictine monastery community of Mount Saviour had been founded three years earlier. What drew you to Mount Saviour and finally strengthened you in your decision that becoming a monk really was your path?

DSR: The only important question for me was whether the Rule of St. Benedict was truly lived there. That was all. Nothing else was of importance to me. I was completely caught up in this idea. That's why I needed to stay at Mount Saviour for only one afternoon before I decided and left again. The next time, I came to stay for good. That first time, I arrived around midday, and in the afternoon, they sent me already to plant squash with Father Placid. That gave me the chance to ask him, "Do you really want to return to the original Rule of St. Benedict here, without later additions?" His answer was yes. My second question was, "Do you have lay brothers who are separated from priest monks, or are all monks considered equal?" (In the middle ages, monasteries introduced the institution of lay Brothers, which resulted in two sociological levels in one monastery. To my mind, that ran counter to original Benedictine life. That's why for me it was a touchstone of dedication to the Rule.) And again, Father Placid's answer to my question satisfied me: "We are all one here and see ourselves as a lay community of choir monks. We have only as many priests as the monastic community needs." That was enough for me. My motivations were very cerebral, but they set me on the right path. I could make the decisive step, and it is a step I have never regretted. Even errors can bring us to the place where we want to be and should be. In fact, the decision had already been made seven years earlier with the image of the judgment of Solomon.

JK: I want to go back for a moment to ask a hypothetical question. In the Solomonic parable, that wholeness, undividedness that showed you a path could also have gone another way. Imagine you had fallen head over heels in love with a fascinating woman, and she with you. And imagine that you had not cared about overpopulation and you had said, "We want a family with twelve children." Might that not conceivably have been a way of living in wholeness?

DSR: Maybe for someone else, but not for me. When I think back, I cannot feel my way into that scenario. From the first experience in Salzburg onward, I was already inclined in the direction of monastic life. Not that I was constantly thinking of it, not at all. I did truly remain open to other things. But my heart was leaning heavily in that direction.

JK: If I remember correctly, in a former encounter, you said, "After the war, I had two paths; either the right woman comes along or the right monastery. And the right monastery just happened to come along first."

DSR: That was more of a joke that I frequently made. But in my heart, I did know: if the right monastery comes along, everything will fit. My question was more along these lines: Does such a monastery even exist?

JK: Reflecting critically at your early days, would you consider yourself slightly fundamentalist?

DSR: Rather legalist, and that later gave me the greatest difficulties in my life as a young monk—of course, for me, Mount Saviour never seemed sufficiently strict or observant of the Holy Rule. I would have become a great legalist if fate had not dashed that in the form of disillusionment. But each disillusionment frees us from an illusion. There simply is no monastery that lives as close to the Rule as I wished, and perhaps still wish, deep down. For example, as a young monk, I spent days, weeks, and months calculating and writing down what a continuously changing daily schedule might look like, because the angle of the sun changes constantly, and Benedictine monks originally had sundials. That, of course, would not have fit with the guests who wanted to visit us or come to Mass at a specific time. But I engaged such questions a great deal. I could still dream of living a stricter observance of the Rule of St. Benedict than is the case today.

JK: That speaks to the fact that rules, specifically the Rule of St. Benedict, gave you stability in those early days as a monk. You seem to have needed something you could hold on to, to structure your own personality, your own life.

DSR: Fixed structures have always been important to me.

JK: Why?

DSR: I think it is a predisposition, even a bodily predisposition.

JK: Because in other things you are also an artistically and poetically talented person, open for art, for the unregulated, so to speak. That is the other side.

DSR: I can see both sides. As early as the war, we were reading Paul Claudel, *The Satin Slipper*.[10] It contains the sentence, "Order is the pleasure of the reason; but disorder is the delight of the imagination." That was an important sentence for me. I had to learn to live with this tension and am still learning to do so. I was being stretched by this tension.

JK: You could embrace both?

DSR: I was not able to, but I learned and am learning that both are equally important: order and chaos, reason and imagination.

Kerschbaumer Alm

4

BECOMING A MONK

1956–1966

I once summarized what becoming a monk means to me in one of those answers that one sometimes gives without even having to think. Two or three years have passed since I have entered the monastery, and a friend asks me, "So, what do you actually do all day at a monastery?" Without hesitation, I hear myself giving this answer: "We stand around the altar and sing thanks and praise. From there, when necessary, we go outside to do our tasks. But we always return to communal prayer as the center of our life."

At Mount Saviour, we pray the canonical hours seven times a day and once at night, as prescribed in the Rule of St. Benedict. We pray the so-called Minor Hours—Prime, Terce, Sext, and None—at their proper times throughout the day, separately and not joined together, as is the custom in some other monasteries. The bell calls us together for prayer seven times a day, even for those brief prayer periods. At each of those hours, the changing light lends a distinct color not only to the landscape, but to the flavor of our prayer as well. From around the altar, our praise of God in community radiates into whatever work we may do in between prayer times. Praying to God, however, is in and of itself "work"—*opus Dei*, God's work—a lifelong process of ever-deepening insight and grateful praising. Through this process of growth, the entire life of a monk consists in becoming a monk.

"Praising, that's it!" writes Rainer Maria Rilke.[1] With this call, he is drawing attention to three things: the calling of the poet, the central task of every human being, and the innermost nature of Word arising out of Silence for the sake of praising—and for the sake of nothing else. Growing into this tripartite truth of poetry, humanity, and Mystery as Word (Logos) seems to me of crucial importance in becoming a monk. Yes, a relationship with poetry is part of it. It is no coincidence that Cardinal Newman saw the poetic view of the world as the Benedictine Order's characteristic contribution to Christianity's intellectual history.[2] The monk is by his very humanity a poet—just like Adam giving every animal its name[3]—simply by being a person whose innermost self is the praising Logos. The life of a monk allows us to make praising itself the center, and to let its energy radiate out from this center as joy.

Admittedly, it is then reasonable to ask, "And how do you spend the rest of your time, in which you are not chanting in choir?" The short answer is that the life of a monk is astonishingly varied. Our two principal areas of work are study and handiwork—that is to say, working with both heart and hand. Our Prior, Father Damasus Winzen, emphasizes the importance of daily manual labor. In our daily studies, we are to use our rational minds fully, but at the same time, open our hearts wide. To contemplative reading, or *lectio divina*, are added classes in scholastic philosophy and theology (with rigorous exams). Some of our Brothers, who have themselves only recently finished their studies at the Benedictine college of Sant'Anselmo in Rome, are now our professors. Each week, a different Brother reads aloud at meals. This way we become familiar with standard works in the fields of theology, science, and the humanities and with important contributions to current periodicals. In our up-to-date library, I can find the latest books and journals in English and German; Father Damasus personally sees to that. He also regularly gives us spiritual teachings, since he sees the role of an abbot not as that of an administrator, but as that of a teacher—and I eagerly take notes, to penetrate as deeply as possible into the *doctrina abbatis*.

It is true that monastic life is not without its hardships, and for me that includes having to get up early (at that time, just past 4:00 a.m.—in sixty years of monastic life, I have never been able to get used to the time of rising.) Father Damasus enjoys telling the story of an extremely well-read young man who—having already written a book about monastic life—became a novice at Father Damasus's former abbey of Maria Laach. He too found the rough reality difficult to adjust to: when the monk in charge of waking up the others—elegantly called the *excitator* in Latin—knocked on his door in the morning with the words "*Benedicamus domino!*" (Let us praise the Lord!), the novice answered not with the prescribed response of "*Deo gratias!*" (Thanks be to God!), but grunted, half asleep, "This is a dog's life!" (He apparently did not last long.)

Since Mount Saviour does not yet have its own novitiate, we novices are sent to Saint-Benoît-du-Lac, a Canadian abbey. The Brothers there speak French, which leads to several small confusions. The young monk who was assigned to me as "Guardian Angel" and French teacher had a stutter. Only years later did I discover that in French, the linden tree is called *tilleul*, and not "ti-tilleul." In the Chapter Room on Friday mornings, we have public confession of minor infringements. I want to accuse myself of having shattered a light bulb, but I am unsure of my vocabulary and instead admit to having broken a matchstick. The abbot considers the ringing laughter that greets my pronouncement sufficient penance for my transgression. (Yes, in those days, we still did have this so-called Chapter of Faults, and we even whipped ourselves in our cells, reciting Psalm 51, while the bells rang on

Friday evenings.) The abbot, Dom Odule Sylvain, is a man whom I esteem and admire. On high Holy Days, he embodies the role of *tres révérend pere*, who is solemnly robed, piece by piece, in his vestments, before we lead him in procession from his rooms to the chapel. On weekdays, however, he stands high up on the ladder as we harvest apples, or lies on the floor of the bathroom mending a pipe—for he is also a plumber.

Saint-Benoît-du-Lac is famous for its tradition of Latin plainchant, and we novices are trained in the spirit of Solesmes, the leading center of the practice.[4] For my entire life, this chanting has remained one of the greatest treasures. In this abbey church, a long nave is leading up to the altar, while in the octagonal chapel at Mount Saviour, the altar stands in the middle, but in both places, it is clearly the central fount of life for the monastic community. In French Canada, I learn to live and love the Benedictine tradition in its richest form. We novices are grateful for that experience, but we are also happy when we can return to our humble monastery.

Back home, our daily work is varied. We do not hire help, but do all the chores of the house and garden, the kitchen, the fields, and the stable ourselves. Since Brother Laurence is the only one apart from me who knows how to milk a cow, I am frequently in the stables and greatly enjoy my time there. I am also responsible for our "depot," the pantry from which the Brothers can request what they need—notebooks, sandal straps, toothpaste, and so on. Brother John from Weston Priory in Vermont spends a year with us, becomes my faithful helper, and eventually a lifelong friend.

All of us take turns cooking. Cooks and kitchen helpers receive a special blessing when they finish their turns on Sunday. In a stroke of luck for my fellow brethren, I am never made "first cook" but only a kitchen helper. (At home in Austria, my brothers and I learned a great many household skills. Mother even taught us knitting and crocheting, but food was so precious that she could not risk potentially spoiling it by letting us attempt to cook.)

The need for constructing new buildings offers many opportunities for my creative interests and for hands-on experience. For the first few years, we sleep in the hayloft; only when winter gets too cold, do we escape into the old farmhouse; but there it does become quite cramped for us all. So, we must build. Fortunately, we do have generous helpers. Some of our volunteers are even professionals, such as our friend Rocko, a skilled carpenter from town. Alone we would not be able to manage. The Boy Scouts help as well, and over the years, we plant fifty-thousand trees together.

Each morning, during Prime, we receive our work tasks for the day. There are sometimes surprising jobs: one time, I am sent all the way to Connecticut with Brother Ildefonse to pick up huge quantities of canned food, still usable but condemned by the authorities after a flood in the warehouse. But my favorite task is housecleaning. There is always enough of this work, and it is less popular with the others. It gives me the opportunity for undisturbed silence and wonder. Just the way the dust dances when winter sunlight pours into the dark hallway I'm sweeping is a thrill:

My broom the mallet
My dustpan the gong. Dust motes
dancing in sunbeams!

At the time, dustpans were still made of metal, and the handles of the small brooms were still wood—today, the sound of plastic on plastic would hardly cause mystical enchantment. But that homely gong tone opened for me a mysterious realm; Rilke calls it "an inner world-space." He writes, "One single space pervades all beings here: / an inner world-space."[5] The outer reaches of space, which we somehow sense, gazing at a winter night sky, evoke in me an inkling of those inner reaches. This experience is behind another three-liner from my time as a young monk, possibly the oldest that I have kept:

While the brothers sleep
Orion stands guard above
In a frosty sky.

Every year, my family visits the monastery for Easter to join our festive liturgy. There is complete silence during Holy Week; we greet one another only briefly. But on Easter Sunday, we sure do celebrate. My grandmother is still with us in the early years—later, my little nephews and nieces carry the light from the Easter candle in a lantern to the cemetery on the hill above the monastery. There we hold a festive Easter picnic on her grass-covered grave.

Our community has many friends. Most of them come from nearby, but no small number also visit from further away. They bring us home-baked food and many other useful things; they also bring their sorrow and their pain. In most households, hardship and distress come only occasionally, but in the monastery, people bring them to us daily that we may hold them up in prayer. We must learn to include these dark sides of life in our praising. Rilke writes, “Only he whose bright lyre / has sounded in shadows / may, looking onward, restore / his infinite praise.”[6] “Infinite praise”—that is a good description of the prayers we chant. Infinite, not only because they take part in the praise that the Logos sings beyond time, but also because praise must stop at nothing, exclude nothing, not even the things that grieve us. That is how I want to learn to sing. I believe that we have passed the hardest test of becoming monks only when we can say, “Between the hammers our heart / endures, just as the tongue does / between the teeth and, despite that, / still is able to praise.”[7]

The canonical Hours have not been so obviously the center of communal life in every monastery in which I have spent time, but in all of them, the altar was the source of life for the community. I consider it a great gift that, unlike many others, I did not have to search from monastery to monastery but instead had such clear "love at first sight" for Mount Saviour. Later, however, I came to know many other monasteries. And as a student, I had known Heiligenkreuz Abbey, near Vienna. It was my spiritual home because, there, Father Walter Schücker, the Prior, was my spiritual guide. At that time, under Abbot Karl, Heiligenkreuz was open to experiments and earnestly considered opening a Cistercian monastery in Tibet. In 1951, however, with the Chinese annexation of Tibet, the negotiations ended abruptly.

I did have the opportunity of witnessing an unusual attempt to found a monastery. Around 1980, I got to know three young men who had grown up amidst the turmoil of Californian counterculture. They had been questioning so seriously all prevailing majority norms and values that they came to a striking conclusion: only as monks would they be able to authentically realize their positions. And so, they simply set out to found a monastery on their own. They then sought an ecclesiastical connection, and first knocked on the doors of the Anglican Church. There, no one had any idea of what to do with "wannabe monks." The Roman Catholic bishop was also slightly embarrassed, but exhibited a rather benign attitude—after all, the three had lived a relatively strict life following the Rule of St. Benedict for years now. They had found an abandoned monastery building and lived there in exchange for custodial duties in the building and grounds. They now asked me whether Mount Saviour could help them in any way. At the time, our Prior was Father Martin Boler. He went to California for several days, found the young monks trustworthy, and suggested that after a year as novices of Mount Saviour, they could become an independent priory. I was to live with them in California and oversee their novitiate. Unfortunately, I still had a few other obligations to complete, and by the time I was ready, the three had been offered positions in prison pastoral care. They achieved remarkable things there, but it was the end of their plans to found a monastery.

For me, however, the experience led to a fateful turn: these three young men now no longer needed me. Instead, their spiritual companion for years, Father Bruno Barnhart, Prior of the New Camaldoli Hermitage, said, "We need you with us in Big Sur," and so began my stay in New Camaldoli, which was to last fourteen years. This "hermitage" was different from the other monasteries I knew. Communal living was reduced to a minimum; we monks lived each in separate little cottages and tended our own gardens. In the one entrusted to me, I planted two fig trees, black bamboo, and nine various kinds of lavender. Before my window—and a thousand feet below—lay the Pacific Ocean. Its silent blue enormity seemed to rise steeply into the sky. Nowhere have I ever found it easier to dive into "the world's inner space" than in the outdoors of Big Sur. But here, too, the monastic community gathered around the altar as its center and source of strength for daily celebrations of the Eucharist.

Once more, in my old days, I was to live in a monastery in which the altar represents the center of life: in the European monastery of Gut Aich. Here, the form of monastic life recalls the image of concentric circles: healing power radiates outward from the altar to the inner ring of the monastic community. Around that inner ring, the village community of Winkl forms another one, as the monastery is in the center of the village. A further ring consists of oblates, men and women who are closely connected to the monastery in the Benedictine spirit but often live far away. The furthest circle is made up of those seeking inner and outer health here. A monastery is meant to be for the Church what the Church is meant to be for the world: a place of healing. There are rooms here to unburden the sufferings of one's soul, but also a health center consecrated to Hildegard of Bingen, herb gardens, a small factory for herbal remedies, and a center for monastic medicine. As early as the third and fourth centuries AD,

Christian monks were referred to as *therapeutes*—healers. Health means wholeness. Health means being one with oneself and with the universe. The word *monk* contains the root *monos*, meaning "one" and "alone," but also one with the community and one with all things. We find this oneness when we find the eternal center.

DIALOGUE

JK: Brother David, your birth name is Franz Kuno Steindl-Rast. How did you come by the name David?

DSR: David is my name as a monk. We were given new names at the beginning of our novitiate. In truth, I had always wished for the name David, because I had read Kings and Samuel on the Kerschbaumer Alm and delighted in the stories about King David. So, for me, David became a heroic figure, which is why I wanted that name. But at Mount Saviour Monastery, we already had a Brother David when I arrived, and so I had given up hoping. But shortly before I became a novice, the other Brother David left the community, and it was not uncommon for the next novice to receive the name of a Brother who had just left. It was my good fortune that this also happened with me. At the time, we could not choose our names, and so I had not told anyone that David was my wish. It was a great surprise and joy to me to know that I would be called David.

JK: You discovered some of the silence of the Kerschbaumer Alm at Mount Saviour, which lies in a secluded area once inhabited by the Iroquois. You led a purely contemplative life there, a life that I suspect makes it possible to experience a different, completely new way of being in time. All our lives, being and time are given to us as an inescapable set of occurrences. But once we discover it, it is like the experience of a wellspring revealing something primeval and incomprehensible. How were you able to experience the phenomenon of time more deeply?

DSR: Guests who visit a monastery often comment that time stands still there—one of the aspects of the stillness, or silence, one finds and cultivates in monasteries. This means avoiding haste and rush, so that ideally one lives in the moment. This, in fact, is the goal of stillness: to help us live in the Now. The ringing of bells has the same goal.

In monasteries, bells are important; they call to prayer. Their very sound is something beautiful and uplifting. As novices, we were trained to stop whatever we were doing at the first stroke of the bell. If you are writing, do not dot the *i*'s and cross the *t*'s, even if you have just put the vertical stroke to paper. Stop, stop immediately if it is time! All activities in the monastery are done when it is time. We gather for prayer when it is time, not when we feel like it. Ordering one's day according to the bells, and thus finding harmony with the cosmic rhythm of the hours, enables one to experience one's relationship with time quite differently.

JK: On the one hand, time in monasteries is externally organized and structured. But on the other hand, within that structure, it is also possible to experience that different quality of time of which we have already spoken.

DSR: I think that it is precisely through that structured framework that one can transcend time and be in the moment. When we are in the moment, in the *Now*, we are simultaneously in time and beyond time.

JK: Why is that?

DSR: We tend to picture the Now, incorrectly, as a brief stretch of time. If that were correct, then it would, in theory, be possible to cut this stretch of time in half. In that case, one half is not, because it is no longer, the other half is not, because it is not ɔnceive of the Now as a stretch of time, no matter t remains possible to cut it in half. But then where is the Now? We see that it cannot be found in time at all. Yet, we do experience the Now. Understood correctly, the Now is not in time. Rather, time is within the Now. Because when we remember the past, it is now; when the future comes, we will feel it not as the future but also as the Now. So "all is always now," as T. S. Eliot writes.[8]

JK: If my life is existence, then it is spread out into the past, which is in some ways always present. My education, my relationship with my parents, my life experience—everything that has happened in my life is present in some way. I can even repeat and revise it in my memory. But my existence also inevitably reaches into what is coming. That is a significant insight: I can give future to past things. I give future to some things, but to many other things, I don't.

DSR: One might say that our experience enriches the Now: my personal Now is enriched by everything I have experienced in the past.

JK: Enriched, yes, but by being open for what is past, I am also in the Now. I open myself to some things and thus give these past experiences a future and new significance.

DSR: ...the possibility of a future.

JK: Conversely, one might also say that the future, meaning what I act on, also intentionally determines my presence, my being, and my becoming. When you decided to become a monk, you were intentionally giving a future to things that had been. That decision then determined all your future becoming.

DSR: Raimon Panikkar said, "The future does not come later."[9] When it comes, it is now. Remember: "All is always now."

JK: If one wants to say something reliable about the Divine, one cannot do so without having had an experience of being and time. Without temporal experience and experience of creation, all faith is baseless and hollow. Therefore, one needs to understand what creation is, what time is—not just philosophically or intellectually, intuitively as well. In your personal experience, what is the foundation of a good faith?

DSR: I would phrase my answer like this: faith is radical trust—trust in life and trust in God. We are here speaking of faith in the fullest sense, not merely "believing in something," considering something to be true, which is something quite different from faith. We sometimes imagine that faith stands ready, like a train we just need to board, and then it will bring us to our destination. But it is not that simple. Going forward in faith is not a train ride; it's more like walking on water. The life of faith is a continual test of trust.

JK: One could say our entire life is continually being put to the test?

DSR: Yes, it is put to the test, and articles of faith—as in a creed—can be hints, possible sources of support and help, but sometimes also challenges to this life of radical trust.

JK: You described your life at the Mount Saviour Monastery community as a strictly regulated daily schedule of prayer, praising God, handiwork, and study. Can you remember any texts that you studied at the time and whether there were any that had special influence on your development as a monk?

DSR: Yes. We studied strictly according to scholastic philosophy and theology. Our textbook was Joseph Gredt's *Elements of Aristotelian-Thomist Philosophy*.[10] Often, we would memorize entire passages and definitions from the Latin, for which I am still grateful today. It gave us a clear framework for philosophical thinking. Even when one understands that any frame is limiting and one must continually go beyond it, it is still an immense help to have an intellectual framework that clearly confronts fundamental questions and sets one on a path toward answering them. It is good to have such a fundamental structure, and for me, that was indeed helpful. After all, the point in studying philosophy is not to read one philosopher after another, but to find one's bearings in the world, to gain an orientation for one's own thinking. That was very important for me.

JK: And that was possible?

DSR: Yes, the structure we were given was the traditional framework of scholastic and neo-Scholastic thought. But even then, openness was a constant subject: one can go beyond the frame. What we can express in words is not the final reality. Reality always goes beyond the expressible.

JK: What spiritual texts influenced you at the time?

DSR: We read primarily the Church Fathers.

JK: Evagrius Ponticus?[11]

DSR: Especially Evagrius, but also the sayings of the Fathers, the *Apophthegmata*.[12]

JK: Was that helpful for you at the time? I ask because these texts originated in the completely different time, culture, and reality of late antiquity.

DSR: That was very close to life. We lived in that spirituality. But we also read many Jewish texts, such as writings by Samson Raphael Hirsch, a great German rabbi from the nineteenth century.[13] Father Damasus, our abbot at the time, cited him constantly. Sometimes, he even misspoke and said, "The *Saint* Samson says...."

JK: You developed a special love of Gregorian chant during your time at the Canadian monastery of Saint-Benoît-du-Lac. This formal way of singing is nearly two thousand years old, and it is thought to go back to the singing in Jewish synagogues. In one of Abraham Joshua Heschel's poems, there is a description of how the world calls for the air to be steeped in delighted songs for God.[14] Gregorian chant comes out of silence and is the Word, sung. What exactly fascinates you about it?

DSR: Gregorian chant has a special beauty due to its position within the realm of music history. It was composed in the church modes; major and minor did not exist yet. As young monks, we studied this rather difficult way of singing intensively. These chants have an unbelievable beauty, and their beauty is what draws me to them most. It is a beauty that straddles the border between the sensual and the transcendental. When I think of the most beautiful polyphony of later ages, such as Palestrina, Orlando di Lasso, or Jacobus Gallus, that is what comes closest. After Gregorian chant, polyphony is my favorite music. That is the secret of plainchant: it is both sensual and transcendental.

JK: Is that due to its simplicity of structure, which leaves space for other things?

DSR: That is certainly part of it. Singing in unison has a special power, but I also love the music of the Eastern Orthodox churches with its rich harmony. In Mount Saviour, we also learned and celebrated the Orthodox liturgy. We had a friend, Father Pilipets, a priest of the Eastern tradition, and we often celebrated those long liturgies together with him. That is also incredibly beautiful, very uplifting, bordering on the transcendental. The beauty of singing, especially, is one of the things that often moves people to visit a monastery.

JK: You spoke of the monastery having many friends that support it. Is that equally true of what we might call the "seat of your old age," the Gut Aich monastery in Austria? People come not so much out of curiosity as bringing their life, their sorrows, their suffering. They find support in the monastery, including through intercessory prayer. This is where I would like to pause for a moment, because prayer and action are often contrasted with one another: Here is prayer, there is real life. This is where we pray, that is where we act. Or along the lines of "All we can do now is pray." What does prayer mean to you personally? Where do you see the help and power of prayer, and how can we pray appropriately without childishly projecting onto God what we ourselves need to be doing and changing?

DSR: Prayer in all its forms does not primarily mean asking God for something. That is how it's often misunderstood. Instead, praying means opening our heart to the Great Mystery—to life, to God. This open confrontation changes us personally and thereby changes the conditions of everything else, as well. The smallest change we make in the great network of the world influences the whole. When we open ourselves to the Divine Mystery in prayer, then we are aligning ourselves with the direction of life. Yes, that is the surprising thing: life does have a direction. Life wants certain things and does not want others. Life wants aliveness, creativity, change, variety, cooperation; all those things are part of the direction of life; anything that resists those things goes against the grain of life. Life is an expression of the Great Mystery. To live is to be immersed in Mystery; and to live mindfully is to pray. By adopting the correct attitude toward life, we are changing the world for the better. In the Lord's Prayer, the first petition is "Thy will be done;" only after that do we pray for our daily bread and all the rest. Therefore, in prayer we should first align ourselves with the flow of life, which shows us God's will, and then have the courage to articulate clearly how we imagine the realization of God's will. But most often, we pray the other way around: "Please, make this or that happen, and if all things fail, well, then your will be done." That's how we too often pray.

JK: You have often said in encounters that—and this was what suggested the question to me—after your parents' divorce, you had prayed a great deal for your parents to be reunited. Now, I can imagine children who pray as you did; who are, in their experience, not heard by God; and then despair completely over God and want nothing more to do with God. In their eyes, one might say God has become powerless. They feel that they have not done anything wrong. How was that for you? Why didn't you lose your faith when your prayers could not achieve what you wished for so strongly in secret?

DSR: I consider it a great gift that I was taught to trust in God from the very beginning. We have talked about that already. This trust became so fundamental to me that it was not shaken even when God appeared not to hear my prayer. Perhaps I would have said what I later heard from a different child: "God *did* hear my prayer, but unfortunately he said no." If upbringing has not rooted one in trusting God, then one is likely to say, "If there is a kind God at all, then he is obligated to fulfill my request." This was not the case for me. Children, who ask their parents for something that the parents then deny them, maybe even a hundred times, do not lose their faith in their parents. Regarding God, it was quite similar with me: I trusted God, my Father, even when he said no.

JK: To return to the fundamental question: What does the power of prayer consist of, to you, if we are not convincing, persuading, and in some way manipulating God? What is it that makes it good, indeed a central Christian virtue, to pray every day and to live in prayer?

DSR: I can speak only based on my experience; intellectually, I might not yet have completely caught up with experience. Energy—life energy—flows through this web of life into which we are woven; through prayer, we can channel this energy in a specific direction, focus it on a goal; the energy will reach this goal and become effective. Only personal experience can prove that. My own experience does so. I can also feel it when people pray for me, and I am deeply grateful for it. I know how much of what I succeed in doing, much of my good health, and much of all other good things I owe only to that God-given life energy that is bestowed on me through so many loving hearts. This conviction goes beyond what I can prove rationally. But are we not considering a topic that goes beyond cold reason? Life is larger than logic.

JK: Nevertheless, in prayer one runs the risk of becoming childish, imagining it very childishly. I don't mean as a child, but as an adult, not seeing how one must change, what one can do to alter one's own life. There is also the danger of spiritualizing problems that are solvable only on other levels. But as a spiritual adviser, you know firsthand that one needs to distinguish very clearly between those. My point is that one should avoid escaping into prayer when what one really needs to do is confront major changes in one's own life. That would be a kind of "misuse" of prayer.

DSR: Yes, that can happen. Rightly understood, praying means facing the Mystery, facing life again and again. If we do that, life will tell us what we need to do. Rilke shows us an example for life's surprise challenges. In his famous poem "Archaic Torso of Apollo," a marble torso confronts us with such immediacy that we are "all eyes," as it were, looking at this sculpture. Suddenly, one and a half lines before the end of the poem, the thing looks back at us: "For here there is no place / that does not see you." And the resulting challenge: "You must change your life."[15] If we really face up to life—be it in art, in nature, or in everyday experience—life will inevitably challenge us to change. Openness for this challenge to change is what matters in prayer.

JK: Human cohabitation always means being confronted with problems and, one hopes, growing through them. Franz Kafka once illustrated it using the example of love: "Love is as unproblematic as a vehicle. All that is problematic are the drivers, the passengers, and the road." So once a problem has been solved, a new one appears immediately. Some people think of faith as a kind of transcendental insurance policy against inherent problems—religion as solving all problems. How do you see it?

DSR: Faith is trust in life, lived new again and again—new in each moment because life is also changing every moment. Faith is the opposite of insurance. It constantly makes us unsure, but in trust, I know myself assured despite feeling unsure. The more I feel unsure, the more trust I need to feel assured.

JK: The Christian religion does not understand itself as a spiritual system of order and insurance, the way some people imagine it—that one can flee from life's uncertainties into religion.

DSR: Religion gives us security by showing us a path to keep trusting in life. There is also so much more to religion than doctrine. That's just a tiny part of it.

JK: More than ethics, as well.

DSR: Community is a part of it. The community supports you and helps you to realize this trust in life. That is always the decisive element: trust in life.

JK: In the nineteenth century, Friedrich Nietzsche had a different image of religion. He was heavily polemic against a Christianity that was nihilistically conceived in the sense of a faith that mistakes itself for being convinced, for holding certain positions, for a dogmatic belief. Nietzsche sees this Christianity as a worldview, religious ideology. To him, Christianity has become a worldview: "Christianity is Platonism for the 'people.'"[16] Even before university, he encounters Anselm of Canterbury's proof of God, according to which God is the most perfect conceivable being. Anselm concludes that anyone who thinks that God does not exist is not thinking of the most perfect conceivable being, since an existing being is more perfect than a nonexistent being. Therefore, God must exist. While this sounds logical, Nietzsche saw through the apparent logic, identifying it as a mere word game and empty idea of God. He responded to this idea by saying, "God is dead!...We have killed him."[17] This thought-up, imagined stopgap deity is misused for political and moral power—that God no longer exists after Nietzsche. Nietzsche chose the atheist path, presumably because the Christian God he knew from his time seemed ungodly to him. I can imagine that in your years of becoming a monk, you, Brother David, thought a great deal about this atheism—which you were familiar with—and about authentic faith in God—a faith based in experience. What do you see as the foundations of such a faith that does not turn in the direction of atheism but is truly based on experience and is not merely a fantasy that I can choose to have or not?

DSR: We must remember both. On the one hand, experience is the ultimate bedrock of faith, and on the other, anything one can say about the Great Mystery, even if it is completely right, is still more wrong than right. That is the thesis of negative theology, which goes deeper than its positive counterpart.[18] In the end, the Mystery is the Unknowable. And if something is unknowable, then it cannot be put into words. We may experience it by letting it take hold of us, but we cannot ourselves take hold of it. When I was studying theology, however, I was thrilled with the profound creativity of statements on the Trinity. I admired these speculations as a huge cathedral of thought. But the triune God does not live in buildings, not even in thought-cathedrals. They may be beautiful and express deep insights, but reality goes beyond them. How astonishing, that we humans have access to this reality at all! Yet, as we approach it, we become aware of the limits and insufficiency of conceptual thought. When our thinking touches that which extends beyond thought, we experience that not so much as touching but as our being touched. Bernard of Clairvaux said, "Knowledge comes from grasping something, wisdom from being gripped by something." The deepest prayer is being gripped, touched in such a way.

JK: But if I want to share my experience of being gripped, or talk about this being touched in a debate in the social sciences—that is, look at it methodically—I need to think about it. It makes a difference whether I invent something, imagine something, or am speaking from experience. I want to take up the example of the Trinity that you mentioned earlier. One can think of it as a thought game, but I suspect that this is not the actual purpose. Speaking of God as a triune God may be "only" an image, but it certainly claims to be based on experience, not the brainchild of a clever theologian trying to unnecessarily complicate Christianity in comparison with Islam. Why would you want to hold on to the image of a divine Trinity, and what does it have to do with our experience?

DSR: A Trinitarian understanding of the Mystery in not limited to Christianity. It belongs to basic human spirituality. We encounter Mystery as the "Nothing" from which everything comes. The origin of everything—at every moment—is a leap from Nothing into Being. Mystery is the source of Being. In Christianity, we call this deepest fountain "Father," because Jesus used that form of address. This "Nothing" gives rise to the fullness of everything. Borrowing from Greek philosophy, we call this fullness the *Logos*—the Word from out of Silence. The "Nothing" is the Silence from which the Word springs. Everything that is can ultimately be understood as Word, because it speaks to me, and I can answer, can understand the Word through responsive action.

We Christians call this Understanding the Holy Spirit. Through the Spirit of Understanding, the Father speaks the Word, and the Word in turn—through obedient Understanding—returns into the Silence of the Father. Every encounter with the Great Mystery has these three aspects: Silence, Word, and Understanding-through-action. Those are aspects of our basic human encounter with the Mystery, but this encounter goes far beyond what can be put into words. We live immersed in the Mystery. This is beautifully expressed in Paul's statement that "in him we live and move and have our being" (Acts 17:28). We are totally immersed in God—that needs to be emphasized in Christian catechesis.

JK: The idea of the *monachos*, the monk, that you touched on above as meaning "being one" or "being at one," also indicates this "being in God." How do we achieve this experience of being at one with everything, and to what degree are we all called to find this inner monk pointing to oneness, even if we are not monks ourselves?

DSR: This call does not come from the outside, it is the voice of our innermost longing. The human heart longs to move from multiplicity into oneness, from haste into serenity, from distraction into recollection, from noise into Silence. All these aspects of our deepest longing are our inner call to monkhood.

JK: How can we realize this "monkhood" in our daily lives? I am thinking particularly of people who have a job and a family—what might the life of a monk look like for them? How can I cultivate this unity that points to oneness with all things?

DSR: Here again it comes down to that one thing: we must learn to be alive in the moment.

JK: What specifically does that mean? Some people understand it as being thoughtless, living day to day, not having a plan...it is easy to misunderstand.

DSR: It means being entirely present in the given moment. Some people, for example, experience it in sports, as that "sweet spot" during a run when they *are* the run. Some call it "being in the flow"—meaning being alive to the moment. It can also happen while baking bread, working at the computer, sawing and hammering at a construction site, doing the dishes, or caring for a sick person. In that sense, a layperson who is consciously aiming to be continuously alive in the Now is a monk, if you will. And a monk who neglects that aspect is hardly worthy to be called monk. Monkhood is not primarily a vocation but a way of living, and its hallmark is being alive in the Now. Monks are not recognized by their habit but by their efforts to live in the Now. That is true of those wearing the habit, but also of those not wearing it.

JK: That represents a unique way of being a human being. Living in the moment is something not many people do. Martin Heidegger described it very well: nature of everyday existence is falling for things—that is to say, I fall for the next thing, am imagining a future, or am stuck in the past. Or I am caught up in what others think of me, what they wear, or what they are doing. Falling for the "oughts" ("I ought to do this, you ought not to do that"). The contrary model is to be present, to actively be, to be alive in the moment.

DSR: Monks, though, can fall for things in this way too. And there is something else that is important: monks live in communities. The hermit, too, belongs to a community, even more intensely, though in a less obvious form. That is why I hope for good monasteries, good monastic communities that manage to put into practice what we urgently need in this world. On a journey by coach, someone pointed out a monastery to Francis de Sales, saying, "In this monastery live saintly monks." His response was, "I would prefer it if you could say, 'This is a saintly monastery.'"

With my grandmother

5

INTERFAITH ENCOUNTERS

1966–1976

How on earth have I wound up in this far-flung place in the wilds of California? In every direction, I would have to walk for several days through gorges and over mountains to find another human dwelling. Tassajara lies at the deepest point of a valley, so deep that, in the winter, the sun reaches it for barely an hour. Over two mountains and a perilously narrow gravel road, we come to these few carefully tended huts reminiscent of a small Japanese village. There are also three somewhat larger buildings. These are the remnants of a spa hotel built a hundred years ago from the rocks of the stream by Chinese immigrant laborers, who also built the road. For thousands of years, Native Americans have sought healing in the hot springs that bubble up here.

But why have I come to this first Zen monastery outside of Japan, given that I never even wanted to leave Mount Saviour? I smile when I remember how much I enjoyed picturing myself twenty years on—say, on a Friday in 1980—standing on the very same spot, and praying the exact same Friday psalms for Terce as in all previous years. The idea that the future might be so reliably predictable gave me a wonderful feeling of security.

My mother had told me that, as a baby, I was happiest when swaddled closely and tightly. Even then, this showed what stability meant to me. What others find confining, I find reassuring. What others find monotonous, such as for hours stuffing envelopes with monastery circulars, I find highly satisfying. I feel safe in repetition; it feels like the mirroring of eternity amid time and gives me support. I was happy and satisfied at Mount Saviour and did not, under any circumstances, want to leave or want change. Maybe for that very reason, life had to teach me that the *stabilitas*, to which I was committed by my monastic vows, did not mean sedentary living, but unbroken belonging to the community of Brothers. It is said that between the lines of our vows, the hand of God writes what we cannot imagine. Although life does not always give us what we want, it always gives us what we need.

Father Damasus, for example, wanted me to accept the offer of a one-year postdoctoral scholarship at nearby Cornell University because it would lead to contacts with professors who could advise us in agriculture and in building the monastery. Professor Norman Daly, especially, was to become a lifelong friend and benefactor. After I had been in the monastery for twelve years, Father Damasus would sometimes send me out to give a lecture, since he could not himself honor every one of the many invitations he received. On one of those occasions, I met the young Zen monk Eido Shimano Roshi—at the time, he was called Tai San—and he invited me to New York City to experience a Zen training in his newly opened Zendo. How I eventually accepted and carried out that invitation is a long story. I will tell it briefly here.

Father Damasus had studied comparative religion under Gustav Mensching, whom he held in great esteem.[1] Thus, when one of his monks was invited to study Zen, he was open to the idea. I liked the plan as well, just not for myself. Even as a student, I had answered colleagues trying to interest me in Buddhism by saying, "Life does not seem to me long enough to enter my own Christian religion deeply enough, do I need to add anything more?"

This was the time of protests over the war in Vietnam. Students who knew me had invited me to a rally at the University of Michigan. It occurred to me to invite Tai San, too, and he had the courage to attend, even though some friends told him that he, being Japanese, might be deported. As a Buddhist-Christian team, we made an impression on the media. In the long view, however, the more important result was that, through this occasion, we got to know each other more closely. We had to live together in a small dorm room, and felt like two goldfish who had spent years swimming in the same aquarium—completely in rhythm with one another. Thich Nhat Hanh later told me of a similar experience, "In Vietnam, we Buddhist monks felt closer to the Christians who were monks like we were than we did to Buddhists who were not monks."[2]

After my return from Michigan, I suggested to Father Damasus that we invite Tai San to the monastery. He came for several days, and in the resulting conversations, the Brothers asked him theological questions, to which he gave typical Zen answers. They kept talking so completely past each other that, when he left, I thought the entire thing might have been a washout. But to my surprise, the Brothers all agreed: "We did not understand his answers, but the way he walks and stands, his overall behavior—he is a true monk!" Shortly thereafter, Father Damasus did indeed send one of us to Tai San, and it turned out to be me after all. So, after two years of studying Zen in New York, I was invited, along with other students of the Zen Study Society, to visit this mountain monastery of Tassajara, recently founded by Shunryu Suzuki Roshi.

Constantly, these summer weeks raise the question of why I feel so at home here as a monk. The daily schedule is very like that of Mount Saviour, but instead of praying the canonical Hours, we sit on our pillows in the meditation room and immerse ourselves in what we Christians call the "Prayer of Silence": we let ourselves fall into the deep Silence of the Great Mystery. Silence unites; very soon, we have become a true community. What chanting in choir is for our community at Mount Saviour, silent meditation is for the monks at Tassajara. In Christian terms, I'd put it this way: In our chant at Mount Saviour, the Eternal Word praises the Father in the Holy Spirit; here, in contrast, the Word of praise returns—in the same Holy Spirit—into the Silence of the Father. In both places, we participate in the same inexplicable Mystery. Later, connecting the different terms of the two will cost me years of intellectual work, but even now I am experiencing this commonality and it fascinates me. In Tassajara, I become conscious of what Thich Nhat Hanh experienced in Vietnam: that our life as monks connects us deeply—above and beyond all our external differences. This common ground is more convincing than all apparent contradictions.

Today, it is my turn to light a stick of incense in front of the statue of the Buddha. Does that not actually go against my religious convictions? Should I be allowed to do so at all? Did early Christians not refuse even to the death to offer frankincense before the likeness of the Roman emperor? Already I am in line and hold the incense in my hand and still I am unsure. I think of those early Christians, and my thoughts run into one another. But then they become collected in a single point: the Roman emperor. What stands before me on this altar is not the likeness of the Roman emperor, but a spiritual master who (very much like Jesus) advocated values diametrically opposed to those of the emperor. Buddha as well as Jesus countered the love of power with the power of love. Both built egalitarian communities to protest existing power hierarchies. If I let incense rise before the image of Jesus, why not before a statue of the Buddha? "Yes," says a voice inside me, "but are we not praying to God through Jesus Christ?" Certainly. But just as the cross or the statue point beyond themselves to Jesus Christ and to the Buddha, so Jesus Christ and the Buddha point beyond themselves to the Great

Mystery that we Christians call God. It is to this Mystery that the incense of prayer is dedicated in the end. Jesus says, "Why do you call me good? No one is good but God alone" (Luke 18:19). And the Buddha does not even use the word *God* because he wants to keep the Great Mystery unnamed. I focus on this Great Mystery and dedicate my stick of incense to it. Now I can do so wholeheartedly.

Back again in New York City, Tai San and I, together with our friends Swami Satchidananda and Rabbi Joseph Gelberman, set up the Center for Spiritual Studies. Our Swami is a guru to hundreds, perhaps thousands of young people. (He also addresses the crowd of 400,000 hippies at the historic 1969 Woodstock Festival.) Often, all four of us participate in his religious events. We develop a tested format for our dialogues: following an invitation from a university—at one point we are even invited to Harvard—we hold discussions amongst ourselves on the first day, while on the second, we are available for public lectures and panel discussions.

An unforeseen opportunity for our little group soon presents itself, one that will prove particularly fruitful: the House of Prayer movement. This call for renewal from within the Catholic Church is driven primarily by women's religious orders. Over the past century, the active orders among them have worked themselves to the vanguard of their respective areas of work. Their schools, hospitals, and social services are of the highest standard. Now, inspired by the Second Vatican Council, however, these orders begin to look inward and admit, we are professionally trained at the highest level, but by our religious profession, we are committed to a different kind of training—a training of our interior lives.

In 1967, Sister Margaret Brennan, IHM, issues an invitation to discuss this project, and her brief advertisement in a religious magazine draws representatives of about a hundred orders to the very first meeting in Monroe, Michigan. Over the next years, the United States sees the creation of countless "Houses of Prayer," places where for days, weeks, or even years, Sisters can live, pray, and "recharge their spiritual batteries" in a contemplative environment. Frequently, laypeople join as well. They read the works of Christian mystics, and Paulist Press begins to publish its series Classics of Western Spirituality, which will go on to span over one hundred fifty volumes. Still missing, however, are living teachers. For lack of better applicants, we—the swami, the rabbi, the Zen monk, and I—attempt to fill this large gap, since the interest in non-Christian spirituality is also awakening.

In the last year of his life, Thomas Merton became another adviser of the House of Prayer movement. Through his encounters with Zen Buddhism, he had become a key figure of interfaith dialogue himself. I once asked him whether Buddhism had influenced his understanding of Christian teaching in any decisive ways. Unusually for him, he did not answer my question immediately. After earnest thought, he admitted that his encounter with Buddhism had made him see our Christian faith with new and different eyes. Since Merton's books have influenced the understanding of faith held by hundreds of thousands of readers, that alone is a measure of how interfaith spirituality has touched even Christians who were completely unaware of the fact. I myself was later to write a book in which I presented the Creed in ways that, as bishops assured me, met the strictest standards for orthodoxy—but also allowed the Dalai Lama to identify with its words and even write a preface.[3]

I was privileged to get to know the Dalai Lama at the San Francisco Zen Center on his very first visit to the United States. Even in this first encounter, he showed me how his deep spirituality found unity in approaches that on the surface seem incompatible. In a small discussion group, someone referred to the emphasis that Christian sermons often place on suffering and pain, and did so in almost lewd terms: "Your Holiness, Buddhist teaching frees us from suffering. So, what do you have to say to Christians, who have been practically wallowing in the idea of pain for two thousand years?" The Dalai Lama gestured as if to say, not so fast, please! Then, with great seriousness, he answered, "According to Buddhist teaching, suffering is not overcome by leaving our pain behind us, but by bearing pain to help others." In these words, he was outlining the archetype of Bodhisattva, who attains enlightenment but turns back at the threshold of eternal bliss and vows not to enter until even the last suffering being has been redeemed. Parallels between this and the Christian concept of redemption were discussed at the congress "The Christ and the Bodhisattva," which Professor Steven Rockefeller organized in 1986 at Middlebury College in Vermont. I can remember a touching gesture made by the Dalai Lama on that occasion. We were sitting next to one another, listening to a lecture by another guest. He takes my hand, pulls the prayer ring off my finger, and instead, hands me his 108 prayer beads. Without a word of explanation needing to be said, he moves the Christian beads through his fingers, and I do the same with the Buddhist ones, throughout the lecture. In such moments, healing and salvation become reality, no matter which savior we pray to.

Healing happens in another similar hour of grace, when in 1972, adherents of many religions meet at Mount Saviour. This first great congress of its kind is known as "Word out of Silence;" it attracts Ramon Panikkar, Alan Watts, Archimandrite Kallistos Ware, Pir Vilayat Inayat Khan, and many famous swamis, roshis, and rabbis. We invite also a group of juvenile offenders from the Elmira Correctional Facility who are serving parts of their parole with us at the monastery; they dance enthusiastically on the lawn with all the prominent personalities. I can no longer remember whether it is Reb Shlomo Carlebach or Reb Zalman Schachter who, during our last dinner together, tells a hasidic story that moves us all because it has become reality in our midst: "A learned rabbi had gathered his students together one evening. So strong were the joy and the love they shared that the master sent one of them to the window with the words: 'Quick! Look to see whether the Messiah has come!' 'No change outside,' came the disappointed answer. 'But, Rabbi,' asked another student, 'would we need to look outside if the Messiah had come? Would we not know it at once in here?' 'Yes!' answered the rabbi, 'but in here the Messiah has already come!'"

What had begun in the 1970s was to culminate at the Parliament of World Religions held in Chicago in 1993. There, Hans Küng provided an impulse for the "Global Ethics Project," which posits that all ethical systems are grounded in something one might call a primeval human ethics.[4] This corresponds to the psychological insight that all religions owe their existence to a basic human religiousness. Human beings can become aware that their innermost being is oriented toward the Great Mystery to which the word *God* merely wants to point.[5] We experience this Mystery in three ways: as Silence, as Word, and as Understanding. *Word*, in this sense, refers to all there is, since we experience it as somehow directed at us: it "speaks to us." Word has its origin in Silence. Unless silence "comes to word," our utterance is mere chitchat. Word aims at understanding. Understanding, in turn, is that dynamic process in which we listen so deeply to the Word that it takes hold of us and leads us back to its source—to Silence. The Cappadocian Fathers of the fourth century referred to this dynamic process as "the circle dance of the Blessed Trinity."

I put that image at the center of my presentation in Chicago. It can be demonstrated that Silence is just as central to Buddhism as the Word is to Western traditions and as Understanding is to Hinduism. (The goal of yoga—a Sanskrit word related to our word *yoke*—is the "yoking together" of Word and Silence through Understanding.) None of the great traditions can, from its own perspective alone, appreciate the Divine Mystery in its fullness. Together, they reflect the "circle dance," in which—using now Christian terminology—the Word, the Logos, comes forth from the Silence of the Father and returns to the Father through Understanding in the Holy Spirit. Of course, all images are, in the end, inadequate, but they can help us, if we take them lightly. For me, this image expressed insights for which the seed had been planted a quarter of a century earlier at Tassajara, had grown through my listening to teachers from many traditions, and now bore fruit.

DIALOGUE

JK: Brother David, you have already mentioned that order, rules, and repetition give you security within the monastery. And at Mount Saviour, in the beginning, you wanted as minor change as possible. But then life taught you something else—seen from the outside, there are probably few monks who will later be on the road as much as you. With that, you redefined the monastic idea of *stabilitas loci*.[6] What gives you support and stability in your many travels?

DSR: *Stabilitas loci* is not a Benedictine formula. It is really a misnomer, since the actual term is *stabilitas in comunitate*, meaning "a lasting membership in the community," and that is what a Benedictine monk vows. Since the community lives in a specific place, it is normally the case that a member lives there. But due to circumstances, I have lived a different form of life while remaining faithful to my community—and what is more important, my community has remained faithful to me. Even though some of my brethren may not have fully understood what it was all about, they still trusted me. This trust is a great gift that I deeply appreciate. I always felt supported, knowing that my Brothers at Mount Saviour trusted in me and their prayers carried me. In turn, I see it as my responsibility to do this trust justice by cultivating that communion with my Brothers that is the essence of the vow of *stabilitas in comunitate*.

JK: The stage of your life you have described here is marked by your being sent on lectures and seminars by your abbot. For example, you accepted the invitation of a young Zen monk, Eido Shimano Roshi. After initial skepticism, you eventually learned Zen meditation in his Zendo, and the two of you protested the Vietnam War together as a Christian-Buddhist team. What was the most surprising experience you had when you were first engaging with Zen Buddhism? In the beginning, after all, your position was rather conservatively Christian.

DSR: One important aspect of my encounter with Zen Buddhism was the full realization that the Logos is the focal point of theology in the Christian tradition. It is, after all, theo-logy: a speaking about God. By contrast, a theology that has the Father at its center would have to be a Silence about God. Any talking would miss the point, namely: Silence. Down into this Silence, Buddhism leads.

JK: How can one describe the indescribable of this Divine dimension, which in Christianity is called Father?

DSR: There is nothing one can describe. Our Prayer of Silence, which has a long tradition in the history of Christianity, is no different really from Zen meditation. In our silent prayer, we immerse ourselves in the Silence of God, the Great Mystery. And in Buddhism, that is as central as God's Word is for us.

JK: Would it be accurate to say that one is diving into the "Dimension of Nothing," into that Nothing from which everything comes forth?

DSR: Yes, that is well put. One approaches this Mystery by letting oneself down into the Great Silence.

JK: But this Divine dimension that we call Father in Christianity is also identical with the Nothing. We have access to this Nothing with our senses by simply not seeing what is there, like the source of a wellspring, the existence of which we can only deduce from the water flowing out.

DSR: It's all a question of terminology. The Nothing is not an empty nothing, but it is the hidden fullness of all possibilities. It is a highly pregnant Nothing, pregnant with everything there is. Moment by moment it gives birth to all that exists.

JK: We cannot recognize, analyze, describe, or grasp it. That is what makes us, with our Western mindset, so anxious and uncertain, because we are quick to equate it with nonbeing and death. We fear our destruction in the Nothing, and that feeds our hidden fear of death.

DSR: This is true also of both Zen Buddhist meditation and of silent prayer. (And, as I said, these two cannot really be distinguished.)

JK: If I have understood you correctly, what fascinated you about the Buddhist tradition was a spiritual practice that exists in Christianity as well, even if it is currently not as alive, or at least the treasure it represents is not so widely known anymore.

DSR: What fascinated me was that this practice was so central to Zen Buddhism. Buddhists do not speak of God, so in my encounters with Eido Shimano Roshi—then Tai San—I likewise would always avoid speaking of God. I would speak of the Abyss of Silence or the Ground of Being. But after a relatively brief time, he caught on and simply started using the word *God* himself. So, he was speaking of God, and I still avoided using that term. For me, that was proof that we understood one another. He made me understand in a new way the tension between silence and speech. When I would try to express a facet of Buddhist teaching as clearly as possible and then ask, "Have I understood that correctly?" he'd only laugh and say, "Precisely, but what a pity that you had to put it in words." And conversely, when he would get carried away and begin to talk and explain Buddhism, he'd suddenly break off midsentence, burst into laughter, and say, "I am talking too much. I'm becoming a Christian!" Yes, he recognized this contrast very clearly.

Around the same time, I met Swami Satchidananda, and he unlocked for me still another dimension of the Mystery, one that Hinduism brings into focus and explores: Understanding. Because Understanding is related essentially to Word and Silence, I suspected early on that it might play the same role in Hinduism as the Word in Christianity and Silence in Buddhism. But this division seemed almost too neat and orderly to be true, until with my own ears, I heard the great Hindu teacher Swami Venkatesananda remark tersely, "Yoga *is* Understanding." In that moment, I was overwhelmed. My suspicion had been confirmed in an instant: Yoga—Hindu spirituality in all its forms—is like a yoke connecting Word with Silence. (*Yoke* and *Yoga* share a close linguistic connection.) If we listen so deeply into the Word that it takes hold of us and leads us back into the Silence from which it came, then in a dynamic process, Word and Silence become joined as Understanding. In Christian terminology, the Holy Spirit is the Spirit of Understanding. Father, Son, and Holy Spirit; Silence, Word, and Understanding; Buddhist, Christian, and Hindu spirituality—it all fits together incredibly well. And it was given to me not only to speculate about this, but to experience it in real-life encounters with representatives from these various traditions. That was a great gift.

JK: Then what role does the Christian faith play today in the network of world religions, in today's world? Do you see the Christian faith as one offer among many, or does it have some unique character or claim to truth?

DSR: On me as a Christian, the Christian faith has a unique claim. As an anthropologist, I see it as one expression of that basic human religiousness that expresses itself in many religious traditions.

We humans cannot get around facing the Great Mystery, so, we need to practice grappling with it. The various religions teach us, each in its own way, how to do this. Christianity, Buddhism, Hinduism are ways of grappling with the Mystery, and for me personally, the Christian way is irreplaceable. To a Buddhist, the Buddhist way is of irreplaceable value. What counts is not the way, but reaching the goal, which is the same for all of us.

JK: Let's return to Buddhism. There is a central attitude here that one could describe as "beginner's mind"—though that term can easily be misconstrued as talking about the difference between inexperienced pupils and experienced teachers. What is this beginner's mind that became so important to you?

DSR: For example, when I approach each day with a beginner's mind, I experience it as if it were the first day. Each time one brushes one's teeth with a beginner's mind, one does so as if one had never brushed them before. Once one tries to practice this, one starts to see what a difference to life it makes—how interesting, how alive everything suddenly becomes. One sees things that one never noticed before. That is why Buddhist teachers speak of typical everyday living as a kind of sleepwalking. A sleepwalker simply goes through the motions of each twenty-four-hour day, but a waking person experiences life in all its aliveness. Being awake in this sense means living with a beginner's mind. Am I not always a beginner? After all, I have never experienced this new day before.

JK: Nor this encounter—we've spoken with one another several times, and it is always new. We always start something new, explore the still unheard. At any rate, I certainly do feel like a beginner again and again.

DSR: That's good, both of us must do that...

JK: ...with a fresh mind. One could also say that the aim is to continuously understand things newly and more deeply from their origins. To plumb the depths of things, seek out their source—and not uncritically adopt the fixed terms, prejudices, and intellectual one-way streets—we need to bracket our opinions about people and things, to set them aside.

DSR: By putting words to anything, we generalize it, stick it in one drawer or another, miss its uniqueness. If I refrain from naming something, it remains pure experience. That is part of the beginner's mind as well: I do not yet have the proper name for this. Once I name it, I am no longer truly experiencing it. Instead, the name comes between what I am doing and my living experience. It becomes habit. The rabbis say that getting used to something is exile. In fact, what was the exile? Was it being in Babylon or Egypt? No. The true exile lies in getting used to our condition. When we get used to something, we are no longer standing on the holy ground of experiencing it with a beginner's mind, we are in exile.

JK: I would like to make a connection with an earlier thought: you have said that you need order, stability, and repetition. How do order, stability, and repetition fit with this beginner's mind, which is always seeking to see, understand, experience things anew, living in the freshness of a new beginning, as it were?

DSR: Perhaps that is the very reason why repetition—so-called monotonous work—is so dear to me. Several Brothers find it boring when we send out our circulars together. But each envelope into which you slip something is new: I have never had this specific circular in my hands before. When we live in the moment, for us that moment becomes surprising and fresh as dew. This insight is possibly also what stands behind God's great promise in the Apocalypse: "See, I am making all things new" (Rev 21:5). If we live and move and have our being in God, consciously, then everything is renewed in every moment. The passage in the Apocalypse does not mean, "at a certain moment in history, I will renew everything—and from that point it will grow old again." Far from it! Instead, it means, "Look here! Wake up! I am making everything new at this very moment." That's the great promise. There is no such thing as repetition, not ever!

JK: It is paradoxical: we live from a wellspring that is constantly renewed, and yet the origin of this wellspring is beyond our reach, is neither visible nor tangible. That is a good description of the situation in which we live. We cannot hold on to the infinite Mystery of God, but from out of the beginner's mind, we can discover that there is something that gifts itself to us continuously.

DSR: The beginner's mind listens at every moment to the bubbling forth of the wellspring from its hidden source.

JK: You extended your knowledge of Zen Buddhism at the mountain retreat of Tassajara, founded in California by Shunryu Suzuki Roshi. You describe a moment there where you were assailed by doubt as to whether you could light incense to honor the image of the Buddha—whether such an action might not actually be a betrayal of your Christian faith. But then you conclude that it is in fact possible. I would like to use that as a jumping-off point to ask, How do you see the person and role of Jesus Christ in comparison with the Buddha?

DSR: In the man Jesus, Christians encounter God in a unique way. The Christian tradition points to Jesus in Pilate's words: "*Ecce homo!* Behold the man!" We Christians see in Jesus what it means to be human, and in his image, we aim to become fully human. For us Christians, Jesus Christ is the point of access to the Great Mystery. In him, the Christian tradition crystallizes—just as Buddhism crystallizes in the Buddha.

JK: Although the two play a different role in the concept of the religion...and in their veneration.

DSR: On the surface, more different even from what we would expect, but deep down, hardly distinguishable.

JK: Buddhism and Christianity have different notions of salvation. I would be interested to hear how you describe those. To pick up on a scene you related: on a panel with the Dalai Lama, one of the questioners noted a distinction between Buddhism, which aims to transcend suffering, and Christianity, which is supposedly enamored of it. This misunderstanding has a long history and probably goes back to a misinterpretation of Christ's sacrifice, in the sense that he bore the sins of man to reconcile humanity with an angry Father God. How do you see Jesus' sacrifice on the cross, and how should it be viewed in comparison with the Buddhist ideal of Bodhisattva?

DSR: On the surface, the two are quite different. But this surface is only the interpretation of a historical event. What occurs in the Bodhisattva and what occurs in Jesus Christ is, in both cases, a radical yes to mutual belonging—to all humans, animals, plants, a yes to mutual belonging even with the Great Mystery. This unbounded yes to mutual belonging is love. Interpretations of that can be very different even within the Christian tradition. In the days when Paul interpreted the death of Jesus as a sacrifice for our sins, that was only one of many interpretations of equal value. But over time its growth has so outpaced the others' that today it predominates in the consciousness of Christians and non-Christians alike. Perhaps it has become so established because the framework of sin and expiation is deeply rooted in the human ego. Later, Anselm of Canterbury cast this interpretation into a form that obviously made sense to the feudal society of his time, but today stands in the way of many people's deeper understanding: sin as an insult to God's majesty, which can be expiated only by the death of a man equal to God. Today, we find this repugnant.

JK: That stems from the Germanic theological tradition of justification.

DSR: Yes. The culture from which it stems has changed, but the formula was passed on unchanged until it not only no longer communicated anything that people could understand but now stands in the way of their understanding. That's unfortunately what happened with this doctrine of justification.

JK: But during Lent, for example, we still sing, *"All Sünd' hast du getragen, / sonst müssten wir verzagen."*[7]

DSR: That is precisely what I mean by the passing on of formulas that no longer fit. It is not that the line is wrong; it comes from an interpretation that no longer helps us today, but rather makes us anxious by the associations it evokes. We do have to open ourselves up to the sentence "See, I am making all things new." That will help us also with interpreting Jesus' death and resurrection.

JK: But the question behind it—I would like to take up this motif, at least—is the question of whether there needs to be a sacrifice. We know that life also means sacrificing. And I do not mean in the sense of a scapegoat or sacrificial lamb, as in archaic cultures, but we may sacrifice our individual needs or desires out of solidarity or love so that others can live well. Of course, when we do that, we hope that we are not just sacrificing but getting something out of it as well, that's clear. But the thought that life is a kind of sacrifice as well is not so far-fetched. You gave the example of Viktor Springer in the war, who took your place, in a sense, maybe not with much reflection but out of a feeling: There are young people here who are in great danger, and I have already lived a part of my life. It is better that I be shot by the soldiers rather than them.

DSR: Of course, but I do not know whether one should impute that reasoning to him.

JK: I do not know either, I simply wanted to clarify this idea of sacrifice using an example.

DSR: The idea of sacrifice is an interpretation; it is externally brought to bear on an event. A guest looks at the parents giving the children all the cherries and only pretending to eat some themselves. The children eat all the cherries and the guest thinks, "How kind of the parents to sacrifice their own enjoyment of these delicious cherries for that of the children." But for the parent, it is an even greater joy than eating the cherries themselves, and they do not in the least suffer—suffering being mistakenly considered the definitive quality of sacrifice. In true sacrifice, the one sacrificing answers life joyfully and gives life whatever it is at that moment demanding. If life now demands that I give my life for others to live—the Bodhisattva idea—then I will do so joyfully.

JK: We know that Jesus grappled with his knowledge in the garden of Gethsemane, in the sense that he knew that this betrayal to the point of trial—for questioning religious authorities, thus tipping the religious system into a crisis and undermining the powerful—would inevitably lead to his death under the circumstances of the time. Jesus as a human being had to grapple with the premonition of his impending death.

DSR: Yes, he does grapple—so intensely that his sweat turns to blood. But he grapples through to the decision to do "the Father's will"—not grudgingly, but joyfully. Joy is something other than pleasure. Joy is the feeling of being in sync with life, in tune with Mystery. One may have all the pleasure in the world and yet feel out of tune with life; but one may, by contrast, be screaming in anguish and yet hear deep inside the music of joy, a counterpoint bass line as it were, to shrieks of pain—labor pain it will turn out to be if one is in tune with life. In the Garden of Olives, Jesus says, "Your will be done." He says this in deep anguish, but at the same time, in joy, in the only joy there is, the joy of being aligned with God's will, in tune with the Great Mystery.

JK: And simultaneously, the human side of this decision is made clear when, for example, Jesus says on the cross, "My God, My God, why have you forsaken me?" Jesus does not die with a smile on his lips, as has been said of Buddha, as far as is recorded, but with a scream.

DSR: The Christian tradition underscores clearly the extent to which suffering is part of the Great Mystery of God. In India, I have seen the well-known, somewhat sentimental picture of Christ on the Mount of Olives in the moonlight. It is very popular and many families place it on their home altars. They call this an image of the suffering God, an image otherwise missing from the Hindu pantheon. It is a great achievement of the Christian tradition to integrate suffering into our experience of God.

JK: In the sense that suffering is a reality of life: to stay in biblical imagery, it is a consequence of the fall from grace, the banishment from paradise. Living also means suffering—being confronted with ephemeralness, with limits, with illness and death—and yet not being left alone in those, not needing to be perfect and still being redeemed. It is precisely the imperfect, the incomplete, the not-yet-whole that is redeemed.

DSR: But suffering is not the last word. We suffer when something that is dear to us in our temporal existence is being destroyed—we lose health, friends, possessions—but this is a wake-up call, an invitation to raise our eyes and look at what cannot be destroyed. Eichendorff put it so well:

> Now suffering, a secret
> and silent thief, creeps near;
> we all must face departure
> from all that we hold dear.
>
> If You reigned not in heaven
> what would be left on earth?

Who could stand all the clamor?
Who then would wish for birth?

And then the most important stanza:

You gently break above us
our castles in the air
that we may see the heavens—
so, I shall not despair.[8]

Suffering wakes us up and offers us an unexpected opportunity to raise our eyes from earth to heaven. A well-known haiku by Mizuta Masahide, a seventeenth-century samurai, makes the same point in a most subtle way:

Since my house burned down
I now have a better view
of the rising moon

JK: Together with Swami Satshidananda and Rabbi Joseph Gelberman, you founded the Center for Spiritual Studies in the United States. Through both the Center and the House of Prayer movement, you encountered a hunger for spiritual experience in the Western Christian tradition. What does the Christian tradition need today to become more alive and to better understand the treasures it contains?

DSR: We will understand the treasures of our own faith to the extent to which we share them with other traditions and learn to appreciate the treasures of their faith. But in this respect, we haven't made much progress from where we were at the beginning. Interfaith encounters seem likely to have a long history ahead of it. There is still much that we can learn from one another. However, we should not blur our differences. It's as with two styles of music: each has its own beauty. Nothing is achieved by mixing them.

JK: But one must learn to understand one through the other.

DSR: I would go even further and say that each of the different spiritual traditions has its strengths but also its weaknesses. Sometimes we can recognize a weakness in our own tradition by comparison with other traditions. The other might express an insight of human religiousness better, or go deeper than our own into an aspect of the Great Mystery. In this sense, interfaith dialogue can be truly helpful, but practitioners need to engage in it, not theoreticians.

JK: What are you thinking of when you say "practitioner"?

DSR: I'm thinking of interfaith dialogue as a task for all the faithful of each tradition who want to truly practice their faith. Living faith, in our day and age, must be inter-faith. If we want to live our faith, we should try to get to know those of other faiths. We might, for instance, start a discussion group whose members come from different cultures and religions. Talking about religion can be important, but still more important is celebrating together, sharing religious feasts or fasts. Could Christians not fast together with Muslims? Ramadan would offer a wonderful opportunity. Christians, in turn, could invite those of other faiths to celebrate Christmas with them. Imagine what this could mean for children; how different their attitude toward other faiths would be when they grow up. This is the primary level on which encounters between religions should occur.

JK: And what of religious institutions?

DSR: Religious institutions do have their justification; they are necessary, but as institutions, they are first and foremost concerned with ensuring their own survival. In interfaith encounter, they can at best reach a kind of gentleman's agreement. Events at which official representatives of different religions meet are important. I've often had the privilege of taking part in such meetings and am grateful for that, but I have learned from experience not to expect much from them for a genuine interfaith encounter. Often, the men and women who participate in such meetings do indeed practice their respective faiths at home, but here, their duty is to see to the interests of the religious institution they represent; or they have put on the hat of an academician and see it as their duty to remain objective and unengaged as they give learned discourses on this or that aspect of comparative religion. Interfaith dialogue can become fruitful only if those with practical experience engage in it, not those whose interest is primarily theoretical or institutional. For this reason, monks who attend interfaith gatherings play an important role; they are interested in spirituality; they do not need to defend any institution.

JK: It seems to me that in a globalized world, a world characterized by violent outbreaks, religious institutions do have an important function: they ought to work toward peace and justice by any means possible. But we can see that that is only just beginning. At the Parliament of World Religions in 1993, Hans Küng made an initial attempt with his "World Ethic Project." Now, however, critics of his approach point out that religion cannot simply be reduced to ethical principles, and religions feel misrepresented. What would be your approach for how religions, whose claims to truth do hold the potential for violence, can work toward peace for their adherents? What insights should religions put forward as institutions? What should they support?

DSR: Institutional religions could start by joining their voices loudly and vigorously in support of human rights.

JK: Human rights began as a process of progress in European history, which had been shaped and shaken so strongly by religious wars. The insight was that the primary justification of human rights should not be made religiously, about God, since that would carry the danger of rival religious truth claims and thus potentially lead to further conflict. This premise gave rise to the attempt to establish some form of separation between church and state, ensuring the freedom of religion. In Western democracies, one is therefore allowed to believe and say anything, but no religion may raise itself up to claim, "It is thus and only thus. Only we are right." Within a pluralistic framework, such a totalitarian claim to truth would be a potential source of conflict. To that extent, this construction of a secular state is a form of progress, not an expression of godlessness. And yes, in Europe, we speak of God less quickly in political contexts than is conventional in, say, the United States, which has a completely different history. That has advantages and disadvantages. It can have the disadvantage of cutting God out of the discussion and even forgetting about God. In today's Europe, I see that clearly happening. But at least it has one advantage: the name of God isn't used for all too human purposes.

DSR: That indeed is an advantage.

JK: Human rights are universally applicable. Hans Küng even starts from the premise that the fundamental values formulated in human rights are espoused, lived, or at least aimed at in all traditions—independent of their different justifications in the traditions. It is precisely that premise that I am attempting to strengthen.

DSR: Yes, strengthening that approach is certainly important for interfaith dialogue. All religions fundamentally recognize human rights, with different emphases. If we made human rights the topic of discussion, this could become one of the most important aspects of dialogue among religions. After all, it is no coincidence that Hans Küng introduced this topic at the Parliament of World Religions in Chicago. I am grateful that I could be a signatory to that original document.

JK: But your previous piece of advice was that practitioners rather than the institutions should dialogue. To this is added the problem that in many major religions, there are no spokespeople whom everyone recognizes. Who can speak for all Muslims, all Hindus, all Buddhists?

DSR: Well, one charismatic leader who can speak for the majority of Buddhists—and, beyond that, for countless millions of non-Buddhists who admire him—is the Dalai Lama. He issued an appeal to the world that outlines a new secular ethics as the foundation of a peaceful future. He is convinced that the solution to problems that endanger our future as a human family will not come from the religions, but from people committed to an ethics that can bridge our differences. This powerful fifty-five-page appeal titled *Ethics Are More Important than Religion* is available, in many languages, for free download on the Internet. The innate ethics on which the Dalai Lama builds is what I refer to as basic human religiosity—the one underground water table, which the different religions tap, each by a different well. If we use the Dalai Lama's terminology, I fully agree that ethics are more important than religion. In the context of interreligious encounter, I have tried to express the same insight by saying that our innate religiosity—the tug that the Great Mystery brings to bear on the compass needle of the human heart—is more important than any of the religions.

With Swami Satchidananda

With Sri Chinmoy and Mother Teresa; Spiritual Summit, United Nations Headquarters, New York, October 24, 1975

With His Holiness Dalai Lama; MIT Boston, November 2014

6

HERMIT'S LIFE

1976–1986

In the sixth decade of my life, the fact that I was permitted to live at the New Camaldoli Hermitage at Big Sur on the central coast of California would become highly significant. The community at New Camaldoli combines elements of communal life and hermit life. As already mentioned, I was invited there and received as a Brother. For fourteen years, New Camaldoli became my monastic home in between my many travels.

There I also learned, to my astonishment, that a thousand years ago, St. Romuald, who founded the Camaldolese branch of the Benedictine order, had developed a model for monastic life that is proving especially relevant in our time. Our life expectancy has grown so much that a young person who enters a monastery today can expect to be a monk for two or even three times as long as someone in St. Benedict's time. While monastic vows hold for an entire life, putting them into practice in one and the same form for so many decades can seem monotonous. But the Camaldolese model offers two additional forms besides the conventional life in community. The first is known as mission, and encompasses any form of service for which a monk may be sent outside of the monastery, for instance, teaching, artistic endeavors, caring for the old or sick, helping the addicted, street ministry, or spiritual counsel in prisons. The second alternative to communal life in a monastery is life as a hermit. Monks can live their vows while switching between these three forms—hermitage, monastic community, or social service. Thomas Merton considered this the most promising and visionary model for the monastic life of the future. I had begun to practice it in my own life, long before I had heard of it.

My many travels and my times as a hermit are closely connected: from early on, I have lived in the creative tension between being outgoing and turning inward. We can measure the degree of our aliveness by how wide the range of our relationships is and how deeply we dare to explore mutual belonging with all that lives. To live fully, we need to honor both poles of being in contact, the inner and the outer. Even a hermit who understands his task does not simply withdraw from contact as such, but merely from outward contact. And for what goal? To renew that deep inner contact without which any outward contact must remain superficial. A short fable illustrates this well: Every year, a hermit retreated deeper into his cave. Mockingly, a visitor asked him, "What do you expect to find in the deepest depths of your cave?" And the hermit answered, "All the world's tears."[1]

All of us need both breadth and depth—travels outward into the breadth of the wide world, and retreats into our inward depth. Rhythm and shape of these alternating movements differ from person to person. For me, it is vital to find secluded places where I can dedicate time to inwardness. Like so many things, this is both a need and a gift—and as a gift, it is both blessing and duty. Even as a child, I would look for and discover places to be alone. One of my favorite spots was a small wellspring outside the village. I never tired of sitting there on my own, amazed at the way the water came out of the ground and listening to its sound. As a student, I would sometimes flee from a party in full swing (as much as I loved to dance!) to the only place where I could be alone: the bathroom. In my summer on the mountain pasture, finding a place to look inward amidst the postwar chaos was just as important to me as the fact that I got something to eat there. As a young monk, too, I was sometimes permitted to spend a day or even several days in a row at the small hermit's cabin in the monastery woods. That began as the result of a dream in which something (I could not name it) weighed heavily on me. Desperately, I would search for a way out, and finally a long, narrow tunnel led me into the open. There I stood, in brilliant sunlight, and looking around, saw our hermitage. We had called it *Porta Coeli*—"Heaven's Gate"—and that is indeed what it became for me: the place of a blessedness that cannot be put into words.

Later, when I began to go on lecture tours, periods of aloneness became more important than ever. Other monks do not always look kindly on this need. The typical response is "If a Brother is strong enough to live on his own, we need him in our community. If he is not, then he needs us." But my abbot told me, "You are among so many people on your lecture tours. When you come home, you do not need still more people, not even your Brothers in the monastery. The hermitage will be good for you." He was right. At first, I would retreat to one or the other of our hermitages at Mount Saviour, then eventually to other fitting locations. Some of them, which I will describe in greater detail later, were quite romantic, such as Bear Island, a tiny island in the North Atlantic, where I was grateful to survive a winter of record-breaking cold, or Sand Island Light, an abandoned lighthouse in the Gulf of Mexico from where I could see nothing but sea and sky. But one should not have any romantic ideas about the life of a hermit. In the end, it requires sober confrontation with oneself and with "all the tears of the world." Part of the hermit's life includes being willingly "exposed on the cliffs of the heart," as Rilke has poetically put it.[2] The outward expression of being exposed to one's inner storms is the surrender of bourgeois comforts.

I had the opportunity of experiencing that on Bear Island, a tiny isle of less than twenty acres, which has space only for a coast guard lighthouse and the hundred-year-old summer home of the Dunbar family.[3] These generous friends gave me the permission to spend the winter of 1976–77 in one of their buildings. I selected a wooden structure with a workshop and wood storage space on the ground level and two rooms above. Dick Dunn, my hermit's companion there, helped me insulate the walls, as best we could, against wind and cold. In the Middle Ages, St. Francis of Assisi had called for a hermit Brother to always have a second one as a companion; we find this practice as far back as the early desert fathers. When that cooperation is successful, it grants the hermit greater outward and inward freedom. In our case, it succeeded, as Dick mastered the art of brotherly care and the even rarer art of making himself invisible precisely out of care.

We managed to keep ourselves warm quite well with our wood stoves; on the wall's top shelf, it was even warm enough to coax alfalfa seed to give us sprouts. But on floor level, a little pile of snow, blown in by the wind through a hole in the wall, would not melt. Obviously, the place was not entirely winterproof after all. During the worst storm of that winter, we had to flee to the lighthouse in the middle of the night. The lighthouse—by permission of "Captain," the cat—housed Steve Cancellari of the U.S. Coast Guard; his wife, Mary; and their daughter, Maggie, as well as their baby boy. We would normally see them only on Sundays, when they would take us in their motorboat to Mass at Southwest Harbor. That could become a dangerous little voyage, as it did on Christmas Day. When we set out that morning, the sea was as smooth as glass, but after the service, the waves were so high that Steve would not attempt the crossing back until hours later. And it was a daring attempt: Dick and I could hardly bail the water out of the boat fast enough to keep up with the waves pouring over the side, while Mary tried to calm the crying children. Despite all his skill, Steve was unable to maneuver the boat to the correct position at the dock, so that we ended up carrying the children ashore through waist-deep water that was cold as ice. We celebrated the rest of Christmas Day in bed keeping warm, helped by whatever alcoholic beverages we could find. And if motorized crossings could get dangerous, they were nothing compared to the rowing. More than once, we thought our last hour had come. But this kind of "sweet danger, ripening" is part of a hermit's life as well.[4]

I got to experience a very different facet of that life in the high desert of New Mexico. There, monks of Mount Saviour led by Father Aelred Wall had founded the Monastery of Christ in the Desert in 1964. I was privileged to experience Lent on my own in an adobe hut not far from the monastery. Over that period, the joint celebration with the Brothers became a source of strength for my time alone because, there, the Hours of Prayer followed the cosmic rhythm of days and seasons, as St. Benedict had intended. Walking to prayer through the desert, under the night sky hung with stars like glittering dewdrops, hearing the coyotes howl around me—that was an incomparable beginning to the day. Then, depending on the position of the sun, different brown, red, violet, orange rock cliffs of the canyon would be illuminated during each hour of the day, until—after the last flare of sunset—dusk muted and faded the interplay of color. This hourly transformation of the light gave the days an outward and inward rhythm. A hermit monk is not supposed to decide on a fixed daily schedule (those who want that can find it in the monastery). He is supposed to remain free to be led by the Spirit that "blows where it chooses" (John 3:8). But this divine breath of life is expressed in the rhythm of the cosmos, and that rhythm will naturally shape the daily schedule in the hermitage, regardless how it might look in its details. The more we inwardly adapt to nature, the more we become capable of resisting the arbitrary willfulness that is so prominent in our society. I became particularly aware of this aspect of hermit life in those weeks that I spent—as foreshadowed by the name of the monastery—with Christ in the desert. I experienced yet another form of hermitage during my days on Sand Island in the Gulf of Mexico—in fact, barely an island, just a mass of rock big enough for a lighthouse. Its tower is 130 feet high, and if you'd lay it down on the disc of the island to look like the minute hand on the face of a clock, it would extend in any direction far beyond the circle of the shore. We—I was with my friend, Franciscan Father Augustin Gordon—had to search a long time before we found a fisherman ready to ferry us across the eighteen miles from Mobile, Alabama, to that forlorn dot out in the great blue. In the end, we did find one who was willing to do so, and he promised also to pick us back up at an agreed-upon day. Despite the high surf, he brought us close enough that we could throw our backpacks on land and jump after them; there was neither a dock, nor (despite the island's name) even a grain of sand, only forbidding stone cliffs. The lighthouse keeper's hut had burned down long ago, and the sea had swallowed its remains. All that was still standing was the lighthouse tower, and we had to climb up its outside to get to the door, which had apparently once led to the tower from the hut's second floor. The spiral staircase was still in quite good condition, so we could get up into the lamp room, where we spread out our sleeping bags. We would meet every evening to celebrate the Eucharist together; the rest of the day we spent on the balcony that circled the tower below its highest peak—each of us by himself in silence, looking out at sky and sea. As we gazed into this distance, more and more "the world's inner space" opened for us, and aloneness turned into all-oneness.

In most cases, the places where I lived alone were far less extraordinary—though all of them became very dear to me. One remains especially dear: the hermitage that I had the honor of establishing with my friend Father John Giuliani. Together, we participated in the founding of Benedictine Grange in Connecticut. We called our experiment the Grange because the word described not only a small monastic outpost away from the monastery but also a storage space for grain; the eremitic lifestyle is part of the grain of monasticism to be stored for the future. For that reason, I had the privilege of setting up a hermitage in one half of our one-car garage. I even put in a ceiling to create a second floor, though that turned out to be so low that one could not stand upright in it. The British poet Kathleen Raine visited me, climbed up the ladder, carefully kept her head bowed, and sat down at the desk.[5] Later, she dedicated a poem to me on the question of how many angels could dance on the head of a pin. I did feel surrounded by angels at all times, but too dramatic an environment can become a distraction. In the most ordinary setting, genuine hermits can reach their essential goal: being alone with the All-One—*solus cum Solo*—following a flexible daily rhythm in harmony with nature, and keeping the heart "exposed" and open to "all the world's tears."[6]

Finally, there is one hermitage where I felt particularly at home: Sky Farm Hermitage. My friend since 1968, Father Dunstan Morrissey, OSB, had received the donation of a large piece of land in Sonoma, California, north of San Francisco, and lived there as a hermit, providing hospitality for others seeking solitude and silence. He called the place Sky Farm, although its stony ground is not for farming and by day, there is not much to reap, but by night, the sky curves overhead like the arching branches of a tree heavy with harvest—a harvest of stars so close you might be tempted to reach out to pluck them. For years, my friends Sister Michaela and Brother Francis had been looking for the right place to realize the kind of hermitage they had been imagining, and I had tried to help them find that place. On the fourth of July 2002, I was visiting with them and again we spoke about their plans and hopes. This time, it occurred to me to write to Father Dunstan: "The two of us are not getting younger. What do you think of the idea that Michaela and Francis might live with you as your helpers now, and eventually take over Sky Farm?" By one of those rare coincidences, the postman who took my letter also brought a card from Father Dunstan to Brother Francis: "Would you send me Br. David's address? I seem to have misplaced it, and I want to give Sky Farm to him." As quickly as possible, the three of us visited Father Dunstan, and a month later, he had signed Sky Farm over to us.

Here, for the first time, I had the privilege of calling a hermitage "home." Between travels, I knew that Sky Farm was where I belonged. We did not see ourselves as owners of the land and the hermitages built on it, but as caretakers holding them in trust and being responsible for this little paradise. We planted trees—olive trees that may still give shade and fruit to other hermits there, a hundred years from now. Land where one plants trees gives the heart a home. Sky farm was home for my heart.

In their own way, the pillar saints, or *stylites*, of the first Christian millennium, who did not venture down from their pillars for years, must have felt the same joy of belonging to a place that I felt. And since their pillars would daily attract pilgrims and seekers, they must have felt the joy of sharing as we did at Sky Farm. There were three spaces available for guests, and they were nearly always occupied. Two of them were huge vats donated by a winery. All one needed for days of retreat fit comfortably in their spacious interiors. Just as we all carry the monk within us as an archetype, we also carry the hermit. Our immense joy at Sky Farm was making those who wanted to befriend their inner hermit feel at home, if only for a brief time. After all, do we ever have a home on this Earth for more than a brief time? The soap bubbles we used to blow at Sky Farm to celebrate Easter flew high above the chapel roof into the springtime sky—and popped. "Doesn't everything die at last, and too soon?"[7]

DIALOGUE

JK: The Camaldolese monks with whom you spent fourteen years at Big Sur live their monastic calling in three forms: hermitage, monastic community, and social service. In your case, over the course of your life, your own calling has taken on all three forms. You were and are a spiritual teacher and travel a great deal. But there are also periods of contemplative life in community and periods of eremitic life. You have said that in hermitage, a monk is "exposed on the cliffs of the heart" and must find "all the world's tears," or at least leave his heart open to them. What specifically do you mean by that?

DSR: That a hermit is fully facing life, not taking shelter in distractions, that's what I meant. And that living as a hermit does not mean fleeing from community. Eremitic life leads those who practice it correctly into deep community with everyone and especially with those who are suffering.

JK: How does it do that? What does it mean that "the world's tears" are with me in the cave, or the hut, or whatever form the hermitage takes?

DSR: Being alone and meditating make us more sensitive and strengthen our compassion for people, animals, and all creation.

JK: But in a hermitage, how do I encounter all that? How does that work?

DSR: From within, by way of meditation—simply because one is not distracted and does not let oneself become distracted. The world is full of tears. Virgil wrote, "*Sunt lacrimae rerum et mentem mortalia tangunt*" (Freely translated, because the Latin is too dense to render it literally, it reads, "Tears, wherever we look, and dying that touches our soul"). Most of the time, we are looking away and prefer to let ourselves be distracted from tears and mortality. But hermits seek no escape; undistracted, they face life's wonders, and all the world's suffering as well.

JK: It is said of biblical prophets all the way to Jesus but also of the early monks in the Scetis that they often had their key experiences in the desert.[8] You also spent time repeatedly in the deserts of New Mexico where one is confronted with an emptiness and with oneself. In the face of such experiences, either one gives up or one grows inwardly. What did your desert experiences confront you with, and what did you find there?

DSR: What I found in the desert was less important than what I did not find. There are no distractions in the desert. That allowed me to encounter nature in a new way—its sheer immensity, its overwhelming beauty, for example, the starry night sky. In the desert, one can see the stars so much more clearly. They appear so near, so large. But in the desert, we also confront the harshness of nature, for example, in the freezing chill of night.

JK: One is also much more grateful for the resources one has available, even if it is only the water necessary for survival.

DSR: Yes, one grows more grateful for all things. And if one lets oneself be affected by that experience instead of escaping into distraction or simply looking away, that gratitude leads to an inward deepening.

JK: Were there any moments in which you thought, "Why am I doing this to myself? I'm in the wrong place!" Are there those moments as well?

DSR: I cannot really remember any such moments. I was always most happy to be alone. The only times when I felt that I did not belong were not in solitude but in a crowd. Fortunately, that happens only rarely, for example, at a reception with many people and superficial conversations. For me, this is wasted time; but time spent in solitude never seemed wasted. Facing everything without armor, naked, was not always easy, but it always felt worthwhile.

JK: What interests me is the psychodynamics in the moment in which I no longer have any distractions around me, where no one is talking to me, where I am relying completely on myself for survival. What is so primeval about this experience?

DSR: Perhaps it is like water becoming still. Everything settles, grows clear, and one can see deeper and deeper. One can breathe more deeply, and something like a cosmic empathy begins to set in. One feels a connection with all things.

JK: One is also in resonance with one's surroundings, the time of day, perhaps with the few animals one sees in the desert?

DSR: Yes. When one has no one else in the hermitage other than a fly, one feels a personal relationship with that fly. I have heard it told of hermits in ancient Ireland that they had friendly conversations with their mice.

JK: And fed them?

DSR: Of course. I'm sure they did.

JK: Can you describe a typical day for you in the hermitage?

DSR: I had no set scheme. "Do not make yourself a rule!" is, from early ages on, the advice given to hermits—do not set a fixed daily schedule for yourself. That does not mean that one sleeps for as long as one feels like in the morning. Basic monastic norms are not suspended in a hermitage. To follow the natural rhythm of the day is highly important. Here, one can consciously experience sunrise and dawn; one feels noon when everything grows still; one enjoys it when the day gets cooler of late afternoon and when evening falls. In a hermitage, one becomes far more conscious of the natural course of the day. Compared with this, the normal course of the day in the city is quite arbitrary; sunset and nightfall do not matter; one simply turns on the light and prolongs the day as much as one wants to. During very short winter days in the hermitage, I did use light as well, but otherwise I preferred to live in the rhythm of normal daylight. In winter, I sleep longer than in the summer. Originally, monks living in communal monasteries did that, too. St. Benedict mentions quite specifically that dinner should be held at such a time that everything is finished before dark. It is important to go with the natural flow of the day; it is much less important how one fills the day. One prays, reads, or writes, does some work with one's hands—everything leisurely.

JK: Did different projects lead you into hermitage?

DSR: There have been times when I have retreated to work on a book project, but I would not describe that as eremitic life. The hermit's only project is being alone and free. Other projects get in the way of that endeavor. Being alone with the All-One, as Plotinus said—this aloneness in and of itself is the project.

JK: And that is different from loneliness.

DSR: Being alone can take a positive and a negative form. I refer to the negative form as being lonely. We are lonely when we are cut off from others; being cut off is the negative aspect. If we feel cut off, we can be lonely amid a crowded room: we are not connected with the others; we feel inwardly cut off. We do not actually have a proper term for the positive form of aloneness.

JK: Perhaps autonomy?

DSR: No, the term autonomy does not resonate with the overtones of vulnerability that I hear in aloneness. (The hermit's vulnerability is part of aloneness. Admittedly, that is not something one usually thinks of.)—*Solitude* may be a better term for the positive form of aloneness, but it may not be all that important to find the precise term for it. At any rate, a lonely person is cut off from community with others while the hermit is deeply connected with them. And the deeper and more encompassing this inner connection, the more authentic—and happy—eremitic life will be. Our greatest happiness, our truest joy, is connection with others. Our greatest sorrow is to be cut off from them.

JK: You mentioned a hermit's vulnerability just now. How is a hermit vulnerable?

DSR: In confrontation with himself. Distraction is like an armor we can put on to avoid feeling this vulnerability. Why would someone want to make themselves vulnerable? Because in the end, it is our authentic state: we *are* vulnerable. One must admit one's vulnerability before one can be open with others in a true relationship.

JK: But at least in that moment, the hermit does not have this relationship with other people.

DSR: Oh yes, he does! Not only with other people, but with everything there is. This vulnerability is not only and not even primarily about the insults to which one may be exposed, but about allowing myself to experience how small I am, standing under the starry sky of the desert, the insignificance I feel there: I am nothing.

JK: But that could also lead me to humility. It does not need to be an injury. Vulnerability, wounding—I sense that that is something stronger and relates with our darker side.

DSR: What I meant by vulnerability comes very close to humility: not putting on any kind of armor.

JK: Could one call that sensitivity, a special kind of awareness?

DSR: Yes. Sensitivity, awareness, compassion—meaning shared joy and shared suffering. The sharing is the crucial aspect. Not cutting off but connecting.

JK: I would like to get back to the darker sides with which we are confronted, so please bear with me for a moment. People are creatures of infinite want. Though most aren't conscious of this, human hunger is marked by its longing for the absolute. However, anyone who tries to still this infinite longing by finite means, making it dependent solely on successful life circumstances, will have little reason for joy in life. On the contrary, there is a high likelihood that longing will slide into addiction—addictive actions or stimulants will then briefly enable a feeling of connection or lift the fear of disconnectedness. Translating the Latin root word *religare* as "to reconnect," *religion* then becomes a different name for connectedness. But back to addictions: they come in many forms, beginning with the addiction to work, which many see as harmless and some even praise highly. But there is also addiction to power, sex, gambling, alcohol, or drugs. Especially in addiction, one feels a lack of freedom. What is interesting is that the Egyptian monks of the Scetis knew this already. In the doctrine of the eight temptations, they called it "the demonic." One is, so to speak, no longer in charge of one's own house. As the Viennese say about someone who is no longer in full possession of their own faculties, "It got him." Do you as a hermit also know such conflicts with addictiveness?

DSR: I've never looked at it from that point of view. I would put it like this: The highest goal of a hermit is to live in the present moment. The desert fathers noticed early on that there are only three fundamental ways of missing that goal.

The first is to hold on to what is past—especially memories. That is always a danger, especially for hermits; one who does not have much else to cling to, clings to memories. That clinging has been called greed and lust, but by whatever name, it makes one miss the present: by clinging to the past, one belongs to the past.

The second reason for missing the present moment is anger—or rather the impatience of anger. Anger in and of itself is simply a strong burst of energy that can be necessary and helpful; impatience is the destructive aspect of anger: one wants to force a certain kind of future and—occupied with the future—fails to live in the present. One would think that preoccupation with past or future has exhausted the options, but we are quite creative when it comes to missing the mark—in this case, the Now.

The third possibility is that one is neither holding on to the past nor impatiently reaching for the future, and yet misses the present moment by not being awake. The drowsiness that makes us miss the Now is what the desert fathers called the "Noonday Demon." In the midday heat of the desert, one tends to doze off in body and in spirit. Spiritual dozing is a great danger especially for hermits, since there is no one around to wake them up. These three "addictions" can make us fail to be truly awake to the moment.

JK: What you have just described, the "Noonday Demon," was what Evagrius Ponticus described as *acedia*, "spiritual listlessness." Evagrius considered this to be the monk's greatest danger, becoming spiritually discouraged, listless, bored. Despondent, one would say. One has no taste for life anymore and does not know what to do with oneself and the world. That may also be a subtle form of depression.

DSR: Of depression or of midlife crisis or of that typical crisis where in the middle of anything one tackles, one then runs out of steam. Acedia is the listlessness in all those situations.

JK: How do I fight that, or rather, how do I prevent spiritual listlessness from taking hold of me? What are the countermeasures to become awake again, or even stay awake?

DSR: Not subjecting oneself to a fixed schedule in the hermitage can be of help here. When I realize that I am starting to doze in this sense, it is time to do something that gives me joy, whether or not I had planned it for that day. It sounds funny, but we must keep on the lookout for things that give us joy. If we fit enjoyable activities into our day, that joy will carry over to all the rest of our activities.

JK: Can you give an example of something that has given you joy?

DSR: Chopping wood is one example. If I have planned to read for an hour but begin to doze after twenty minutes, I can go outside and chop firewood. That gives me joy and wakes me up. Or I may take a brief walk (taking walks is part of my life in the hermitage). When I feel lazy, it helps me to do something that is long overdue because I kept delaying it. My inclination to postpone is due to laziness in the first place. Acedia is laziness. Its first symptom should alert me to counteract my laziness.

JK: Your time on the small islands must have been especially challenging. Sand Island, for instance, is a pile of rocks, and on them, an abandoned lighthouse. You and your Franciscan Brother had to have yourselves brought there by boat. How can one do that, two people being alone in the same place?

DSR: On Sand Island, there was enough space to spend the entire day alone on two different sides of the balcony without seeing one another. Then we would celebrate the Eucharist together. But we would eat alone again. The Eucharist was our time of community.

JK: Though there are few classical hermits today, that way of life does seem to be very attractive: retreating to an isolated hut in the mountains, living in the wilderness in a tent or under a tarp, exposed to the elements—plenty of individuals keep looking for that. There are also new offers that take up old spiritual traditions such as the vision quest, initiation rites, and so on. What, in your opinion, are these people looking for or finding?

DSR: I believe that they are looking for and—when successful—finding exactly what other hermits search for and find. Today, there are few who live their entire lives as hermits, and maybe there never were very many. But temporary hermitage has almost become a necessity for many people in our society. Some go hiking on their own, others have a hut or a dwelling where they stay all alone, and there are also monasteries that make hermitages available for a time. Conscious solitude probably always has spiritual overtones, whether it occurs in a monastic environment or during a hike through the mountains. For human beings, solitude is always an opportunity for encountering the Great Mystery. Sustaining that aloneness for an entire life is indeed something quite unusual. It might be one's special vocation. For me, in any case, it was not.

JK: You needed the rhythm, the dynamics of aloneness, community, and being able to work with people?

DSR: Yes. Many people today—and not just monks—find that they can serve their community best if they intermittently retreat, collect themselves, and find themselves. They have more to give that way.

JK: From the vantage point of the hermitage, one can, it seems, develop an unbiased view of the society in which one is living. Like Henry David Thoreau, who developed his criticism of American society in the nineteenth century when he was living as a hermit.[9] That was powerful, and it became one of the foundational texts of the hippie movement in the late 1960s.

DSR: I've gone on pilgrimage to Walden Pond, where Thoreau lived as a hermit for a time. Unfortunately, his hut is no longer standing.

JK: And how was that?

DSR: I found it a moving experience. Thoreau's spirit is still present there in the woods by the pond. My first visit to Walden Pond happened to coincide—if there are such things as coincidences—with the first Earth Day. That was in 1970.

JK: He was, in the best sense, an incredibly anarchistic thinker.

DSR: In fact, he was imprisoned for it briefly. He took a good look at the society of mid-nineteenth-century Massachusetts and was disgusted by its fake and sham. Later, he wrote, "I went to the woods because I wished to live deliberately." I take this to mean, "I wanted to become real." And becoming real is the challenging task of any hermit. In the children's classic *The Velveteen Rabbit*, the toys on the nursery shelf have one great desire: they all want to become real. We humans, too, have a deep longing to become real. The toys asked one of them, the wise old rocking horse, "Does it hurt to become real?" A hermit will understand the answer: "The more real you become, the less you mind that it hurts."

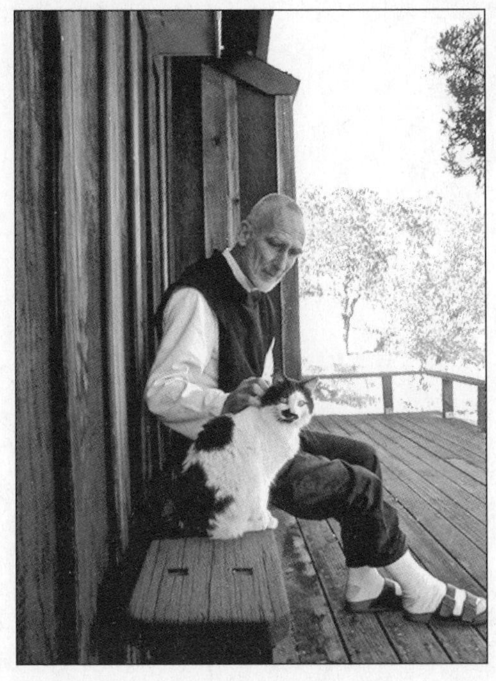

7

ENCOUNTERS IN TRAVEL

1986–1996

Though my longest lecture tours fall only in the seventh decade of my life, I've enjoyed traveling all my life. In my youth, our greatest excitement was backpacking—tramping for days, even weeks, with our heavy backpacks. Since my birthday was during the summer holidays, I was always away from home on this day. My mother's comment was merely, "Well, you are my little gypsy."

Leaving and breaking off all ties with the home was a way of articulating our independence, and independence was important to us. I still marvel at how generously my mother allowed me that independence and even encouraged it. How difficult it must have been for her! On a backpacking trip, my brothers and I were no less cut off and unreachable than Scott or Amundsen had been at the South Pole. In an emergency, we would probably have been able to telephone, even half a century before cell phones. Fortunately, nothing ever happened to us that we considered an emergency; and so, from a departing hug to the joyful greeting weeks later, my mother knew nothing of us or our whereabouts.

A typical backpacking trip in my early teens—we are traveling to the Bohemian Forest—starts by train. The train ride itself is an adventure, particularly on the little local train we change to at Regensburg. Sharp tongues claim that the tracks of this line do not run exactly parallel, and so the wheels are not fully screwed on, in order that the train can adjust to the changing gauges. Certainly, that is what it feels like when the train rattles and sways into motion—though not very fast. In fact, a sign was supposedly posted somewhere: "Picking wildflowers is not permitted while the train is in motion." And there are plenty of wildflowers around the little village where we get off and start our hiking; it is called Zwiesel, if I remember correctly. Backpacking is illegal—except with the Hitler Youth—but no one but us is hiking here, and we feel safe in this remote area. In any case, we keep secret anything having to do with our hikes. Most of the time, we come here with sworn friends from the *Neulandschule*, but this time it is just my two brothers and I. Max is thirteen, Hans is fourteen, and I am sixteen. It is not long until we are deep in the silence and fragrance of the forest. For days, we wander through seemingly unending stretches of blueberry bushes. We carry hardly any food in our packs—there is no food one can buy—and the berries are our main source of nourishment. Only once or twice a day do we pass a human habitation, a forester's or charcoal burner's hut maybe. Then we send in Maxi, our hungry-looking youngest brother, to ask for directions. Admittedly, we do have a map, but we also have ulterior motives: "If they give you something to drink," we tell Max, "you can drink it, but if they give you bread, you must put it in your pocket and share with us." Our method proved highly successful.

Deep in the forest, we reach the barren loneliness of the high moors and then the mountains. One of them is called the Arber. Just below its peak—as with other mountains close by—there is a small mountain lake. Bathing in that icy water is a test of our courage. At night, we sleep in tents. When our group is larger, four of us carry one side each of the *Kohte*, which when assembled in the evening can sleep up to a dozen of us.[1] Inside, we can build a fire and cook in a large pot. Then, by the light of the fire, we sit around the pot and eat directly out of it. For this reason, we carry long spoons that we call "Puszta spoons."[2] The smoke escapes through an opening in the tent, though it also rains in through the same opening if we are not quick enough to extinguish the fire and close the smoke hatch. This time, however, it is only three of us, so a small tent is enough; we are used to sleeping in cramped quarters. On another trip to the Bohemian Forest, six of us once had to sleep in a forest chapel that was so small that if one of us turned over in his sleep, all the others had to turn as well. If the weather is good, we three brothers simply sleep under the stars. When we pass villages, farmers will often let us sleep in the hayloft. We even carry an impressive letter of recommendation from our local cardinal and archbishop—which becomes important during one of our rides. I am sick with a fever, and the concerned local pastor diagnoses, "His pulse is racing!" He allows me to sleep in a real bed in the parish house until I am better, even with a real quilt. Then we walk on. Mother does not need to know.

A highpoint of our time in the Bohemian Forest is a visit to the home of our friend, my classmate at *Neulandschule*, Rupert Steinbrenner, at Winterberg. Though we arrive unannounced, Rupert's mother takes us in like family, and we feel completely at home—for once, at home with sisters. This is new to us, and we are thrilled. After the privations in the forest, we are being spoiled, experiencing home away from home. Might we have had something like homesickness? We would never admit it, but there are a few tears when we depart. Until then, everything is one long celebration here, a celebration of our young life, with flirtation, laughter, and music. We were even greeted with music fluttering out of an open window when we first arrived: a melody from Bach's *Notebook for Anna Magdalena*, which the youngest girl was practicing on the piano. For my brothers and me, this piece remains to this day the quintessence of our visit to Winterberg and those days of unforgettable *joie de vivre*.

We also pass through other towns: Krumau, Prachatitz, Rosenberg—these are the names I remember. When we arrive at a town, we go into the church, pray, and look at the statues of the saints. We have a powerful sense of belonging to this great family, the Communion of Saints. We feel at home in the churches and curiously eye each little detail. On a hand-carved wooden pew—in Prachatitz, I think—we read, "Beware of cattes not so kinde, who woo in fronte and scratch behinde!" We love such discoveries and continue to laugh about the archaic spelling for a long time. Aside from church visits and overnight stays, we never stop where there are people. Even in the big cities of Regensburg and Passau we only stop to look at churches—the famous ones of which we have seen pictures. Then we wander downstream along the Danube, always as close as possible to the river, along the ancient towpath, where men and mules used to pull barges upstream using ropes. For us, those are marvelously unobstructed walking paths.

Suddenly, we see a steamboat not far ahead of us about to cast off. As quickly as our heavy boots and backpacks allow, we run toward the boat. The men aboard laugh understandingly and wave. Maxi is the last one to reach the gangway just as it is being hauled in; luckily, he does not fall into the Danube but onto the boat. We are not taken far, but we are let off the boat near where raftsmen are at work. Laughing, they accept our offer to "assist" them and as a reward we are allowed to ride along on the raft the next morning. In Krems, the raft is taken apart, but we have the opportunity of buying the lifeboat. We are astonished by how little the raftsmen ask for it, but as soon as we get in, we realize that with three of us in it, the boat takes in so much water that two of us are completely occupied just bailing it out. The third steers, as well as can be managed. We are cornered worryingly by an oncoming steamboat on one side and the shore on the other.

After the danger has passed, we see a small chapel on the banks and, knees still weak, we stop there to say prayers of thanks.

After spending one more night—not very dryly—on a little island overgrown by reeds, we arrive at Nussdorf, tow our skiff to land, and sit on the riverbank. From our boat waves a sign: "Firewood, for sale." In these early war years, wood is rare, so we are able to sell our boat quickly and without a loss. Back then we experienced everything that I would later see as significant aspects of travel; independence ranked high, but was never again as important as in those years in which we were first allowed to taste it.

The richest gifts on my travels remained the encounters—just as meeting people on our youthful adventure trips had enriched our lives forever. Each future journey would also bring again hospitality, fun, surprises, wonder, and the unavoidable tears of homesickness and farewell. Each of these key words brings to my mind experiences from my later travels. Let me offer just a few of them, like snapshots.

Many of my most important encounters started during a course called "Spirituality for Our Times," which in the 1980s, I presented annually at the Jesuit university of St. Louis, Missouri. The overall program was called "Focus on Leadership," and many of the participants had been heads of religious orders who were now able to devote a year to furthering their spiritual education after their terms had expired. They came from Asia, Africa, Australia, and other parts of the world and often wished that the other members of their order could hear the program. Consequently, I was invited to all parts of the globe; soon receiving more invitations than I could accept.

For example, the Sisters of St. Joseph of the Sacred Heart wanted me to meet all of the over one thousand Sisters of their Australian order. On the vast continent of Australia, this involved a journey of over six thousand miles, since often only two or three of the "Brown Joeys" (their nickname was based on the Australian term for baby kangaroos) were serving God's people, hundreds of miles from their nearest Sisters. In Australia's Northern Territory, I was flown by a bush pilot into Turkey Creek—a village consisting of only one building, namely the schoolhouse, and five huge fires around which the Aborigines lived out in the open air. As soon as I landed, the two Sisters on mission here took me from fire to fire and introduced me to the chiefs. The government had erected the school, where the Sisters were expected to cover the same lesson plan as in the city schools of Sydney. Instead, they dealt more creatively with the situation: they taught the children—or actually the mothers and their children—to avoid generational conflict, not in the schoolhouse but outside in an airy bough shed, and adapted the lesson plan to the circumstances as much as possible. I will never forget the encounters with the children, who gave me drawings they had made, or with their mothers, or especially with the wise elders of the tribe. Nor will I forget the many brave Sisters of the order on their lonely outposts.

I have experienced such frequent and such openhearted hospitality on my travels that it is difficult to select individual examples, but Polynesia is famous for its almost reckless overwhelmingly heartfelt hospitality. I experienced this in Apia, the capital of Samoa, where Cardinal Pio Taofinu'u had invited me to hold a retreat for all the priests of his diocese.[3] The Cardinal sat in their midst, wearing nothing but a cardinal-red loin cloth, and for an entire weekend, proved to me that Samoan hospitality deserves its fame. The people of Tonga, however, are no less hospitable. Once, Irish monks who had founded a monastery in New Zealand and had a host of novices from Tonga invited me to help them deal with an unusual challenge: When guests from their homeland visited the monastery, the Tongan Brothers knew no higher rule than hospitality. The singing and dancing continued half the night, and the next day all the monastery's refrigerators were empty. The novices had used up anything that was edible or drinkable. In their defense, they cited the Rule of St. Benedict:

"Guests should be received as Christ himself." "Well, this is how we would receive Christ in Tonga," they would say, and I did not know which to admire more: the hospitality of my Tongan Brothers or the patience of the Irish ones.

In Nigeria, my host, with innocent determination, forced a guest gift on me that would get me into quite amusing troubles. A chief insisted on presenting me with an elephant tusk engraved with a personal dedication. Shocked and dismayed, I refused as desperately as gratitude would allow, but to no avail. Then the huge tusk did not fit into my suitcase; I had to wrap it in newspaper and tie it to the outside. My hopes that Nigerian officials might notice and confiscate it turned out to be wishful thinking. Walking through Munich airport, I heard outraged whispers behind me, and I pleaded with customs officers to impound this contraband—again, to my amazement, to no avail. In the end, I asked some Bavarian nuns to sell the ivory to benefit the poor and felt blissfully relieved when I was finally rid of it. Two months later, now home at Mount Saviour, I received the proud message that one of the Sisters—to surprise me (and she sure did!)—had succeeded in smuggling that thing into the United States under the long skirt of her habit.

However, there were also more pleasant surprises. When I arrived in Kenya, I had no idea that a series of lectures I was to give had been canceled at short notice. But Japanese friends who just happened to be in Nairobi at the time had found out that my schedule was free. They awaited me at the airport and took me on several days of safari, with lions, zebras, giraffes, and the overwhelming view of Mount Kilimanjaro. I cannot say what amazed me more: such beauty of nature or the variety of human encounters.

Often, I encountered audiences who wanted to hear me speak about happiness or peace and justice, but were not particularly interested in the Christian message, sometimes even opposed to it. My very first seminar at Esalen Institute is a good example. The program director there knew me from having been one of the teachers that Stan Grof invited to give presentations during his month-long seminars. One Saturday morning, I got a call at the Big Sur monastery requesting if I could quickly come down and take over from a teacher who had failed to show up for his weekend workshop. In the car, rushing down the hill to be on time for the morning session, I remembered that I had not even asked what topic I was to speak on. I was in for a surprise. The topic was "Why I am *not* a Catholic." Well, I was able to start out with some good reasons I myself could find. Fortunately, not one of the participants walked out on that monk who popped up in place of the disgruntled ex-priest they expected, in fact, a good many came back for later seminars I gave on other topics. The titles I chose were designed to lead to encounters with a wide variety of people—Prayer, Christian Mysticism, but also Science and Spirituality with Fritjof Capra, Pier Luigi Luisi, or Rupert Sheldrake, Hiking and Poetry with Steve Harper, and what came to be known as our "Film Festivals," which my dear friend and colleague Francis Lu and I "celebrated"—that seems to me the appropriate term—for more than a quarter of a century.

In fact, some of my most enjoyable encounters were with coleaders—so with the Tai Chi master Cungliang Al Huang; with great enthusiasm, we did "Poetry East/West" together. With Malidoma P. Somé, a great West African teacher, who had been traumatized by his mission-school experiences, I co-led a workshop in which we experienced deep healing and forgiveness—besides dancing to his drumbeat for a whole night without getting tired. With Roger Grande, a pioneer of Thai massage in the West, I gave a workshop on "The Pleasure of Touching" and "The Joy of Being in Touch," and with the Russian psychiatrist Vladimir Lutchkov, a weekend with the tongue-in-cheek title "Authority—from the Perspectives of the Kremlin and the Vatican."

Still more exotic encounters provided a memorable pilgrimage with the Sisters of Compassion in New Zealand. A hundred years earlier, their foundress, Mother Marie-Joseph Aubert, had dedicated the order to serving the Maori—against significant resistance from white settlers. Now, the descendants of these Maori people were showing their gratitude: to celebrate the centenary of the founding of the order, they hosted more than a hundred Sisters on a ten-day pilgrimage up the Wanganui River from village to village where Mother Aubert had founded schools. We walked all day, and each evening, we were received at a different *marae*[4] with impressive festivities. We pilgrims would gather at the gate to the *marae* and wait until women inside—only women have this right—invited us with song to enter their sacred precinct. Then, young warriors in grass skirts made ceremonial mock attacks on us. There followed long speeches and response speeches between arriving guests and waiting hosts. Finally, an elder among us pilgrims placed a fern leaf on the ground between the two groups. Only after our hosts picked up this sign of peace, were we officially accepted as welcome guests. Forming a long line, we exchanged the nose kiss, or *hongi*, with everyone from the young warriors to the last snotty baby a mother held up. From that moment, we were simply family members, uncles and aunts, to the children. Our hosts dined us lavishly and put us up to sleep in the longhouse between the carvings of the ancestors. (Along the entire way, Maori children helped me gather trash. From the north of Scotland to near the South Pole, I have been able in this way to clean up Mother Earth.)

In India, I was to experience the surprises of a different kind of pilgrimage. Father Bede Griffiths, whom I was visiting at Shantivanam—his monastery that is also an ashram—entrusts me to his friend, a Hindu priest, who takes me on a pilgrimage through the south of India—on foot, by train, and by oxcart. In Chidambaram, where we meet not a single non-Indian person, we participate in a highly festive *Puja*[5] in one of India's holiest temples; both Shiva and Vishnu are worshiped here. Almost more touching is the attitude of a young temple priest in the Kali temple on the city's outskirts: the humility with which he encounters the poor. When we arrive in Pondicherry, Shri Udar Pinto, one of the pioneers of the experimental international city Auroville, furrows his brow at the red mark on my forehead. I, in turn, feel foreign in this French enclave and am homesick for true India. Neither here nor on any of my other journeys do I want to be a tourist, much less an anthropologist. I simply want to be a brother among sisters and brothers of the human family.

In Taiwan, I encounter people high up in the restricted mountain areas—a rare privilege accorded to me because I have been invited here by Maryknoll Fathers. I am fascinated by the appearance of the tall, young indigenous women, now nuns, striding like white-robed queens. In my youth, headhunting was still practiced here. One day, an indigenous catechist with whom I became friends appears very sad. "How far you have come," he explains through our interpreter, "and now we do not even have a common language." I search for an answer. Then I remember: "But we can drink together." He likes the idea. To him, it means drinking from the same vessel, cheek to cheek. The rice wine tastes like petroleum, but the ritual touches me deeply. Then my friend says solemnly, "In the old days, one did that only once in life."

Is not everything in this life, if done with full awareness, done only once? Is not life a journey of encounters? Is not all suffering on the road homesickness, and is not this homesickness in the end a homesickness for God—for finding shelter and protection in the Great Mystery?

DIALOGUE

JK: "You are my little gypsy," is something your mother apparently said to you when you once again went on an adventure tour to the Bohemian Forest. The seventh decade of your life is likewise shaped by lengthy tours for seminars and lectures all over the world. You have been invited often. The title of this phase of life is headed by the word *encounters*. When we travel and encounter someone in foreign parts, then on the surface it is at first a form of contact with something new, something strange, one might say. What were the central insights and experiences that your travels made possible?

DSR: Possibly, my most important discovery was that, in moments of true encounter, we feel a deep inner connection with people who, outwardly, are completely different, even in their views, culture, and way of life. A spark jumps over and we are one with each other. One example comes to mind: I was traveling in India at the time, before Indian Airlines had begun using computers. Often one had to call or send a telegram to secure a connecting flight. I was stranded in Madras, the city known today as Chennai. I had an Indian Airlines ticket to Calcutta and needed a connecting ticket from there. But it was rather obvious that the official trying to sell me the ticket wanted to be bribed, which I would not do out of principle. So, he made me go to his office, wait, come back the next day, and again the next. He sent a telegram, and that cost something. Then he made phone calls, and they cost something as well. Then, in the end, he wanted to sell me a suspicious connecting ticket. After all this waiting, I was already somewhat worn down, but suddenly something inside me changed and I said to him, "Imagine yourself in my shoes. If you were me and I wanted to sell you this ticket, would you buy it?" At that, he fell out of his role completely and said, "Under no circumstances. That is not a good idea. But I will help you." From that point on, everything was settled quickly. He knew exactly what he needed to do and did not ask for any more money. Everything worked perfectly. Unfortunately, I have not managed to do that very often in my life. But for me it is always a significant experience to encounter a stranger in such a way that something shines out in both of us. When that happens, the charade is over and a live encounter takes place. Aliveness is mutual connection. Where that is missing, the best we can manage is polite play acting. The most beautiful experiences on my travels are moments when strangeness switches over to connectedness.

JK: Your travels often bring you into contact with more elemental religions, such as the indigenous tradition in the United States, but also in Taiwan, New Zealand, and Australia. You are trained in ethnology and religious studies—both open to and curious about the things other traditions can give us. What kinds of horizons did these religions open for you? What were you able to learn from them?

DSR: What touched me most whenever I encountered archaic religions is the people's sense of the holiness of everyday life. The separation between the sacred and the profane is not as distinct as it is for us. People are conscious of "Mana," of the presence and power of Mystery in everything. I would compare this sensitivity for the Holy to a stronger sense of vision, an ability to look through things and see their transcendent aspect. The Holy evokes both awe and fascination when one encounters it in things such as lighting a fire, sowing seed, or preparing food. Drawing water, boiling it, making tea—such simple, everyday activities suddenly become holy acts before our eyes. In India, unfortunately, this consciousness has largely disappeared in recent decades. My memories are still of the early 1970s, and back then, when I walked anywhere in India, I felt as if I were in a cathedral. Every place in that country felt like a holy site. Even in the cities at that time, at every corner people performed sacred actions, decorated altars, honored images of deities. All day long, they did whatever they had to do, with a sense of reverence. I hope that might still be the case today in the tens of thousands of Indian villages. But in the cities, the sense of the Holy seems to have been largely lost.

JK: You described some of the places where you were welcomed, such as a South Sea island. You recalled that the feature of these societies that most stood out was hospitality. Everything is shared, even if there is little to go around. Is hospitality something that you miss in our culture? Is that something we can learn from these people?

DSR: Well, I have also experienced a great deal of hospitality in our own culture. But the difference may be that, for us, hospitality is quite selective—not just toward strangers but also toward other social circles. Most people move rather exclusively within their own class and social circle, and that is as far as hospitality extends. I notice this in our society, and in India, it is still far more pronounced: for all practical purposes, India still largely maintains the caste system. But there are still cultures that practice an all-embracing hospitality; an essential feature of their hospitality is that it is not selective. To Maoris, for instance, it does not matter whether you are black or white, rich or poor, or different in some other way. What matters is that you are a stranger, one left alone, without the support of family or friends. That is enough to trigger hospitality.

JK: That reminds me of Jesus' words: "I was a stranger and you welcomed me" (Matt 25:35)—though mirrored in a different culture.

DSR: Yes, this hospitality is simply the expression of innate human compassion.

JK: Hospitality without distinctions. But sometimes cultural differences can also lead to difficult moments. You related how in Nigeria you were given an entire elephant tusk, engraved with your name, as a guest gift. You tried to resist as best you could, but out of politeness, finally had to take it, and tried in vain to give it away. Hospitality can have its pitfalls as well.

DSR: Yes, and hospitality can be painful as well. I once felt its pain when I was hosted by extremely poor people. Their hospitality was so lavish that they did not simply share their own daily bread with me, no, they went out to buy me things they would never get for themselves—and which, in fact, I don't like, such as Coca-Cola and potato chips. I felt deeply grateful, but I also felt pain. Gratefulness can encompass pain.

JK: One wants to give something back and cannot. On one of your trips to India, you also visited Bede Griffiths in his ashram, Shantivanam. What did you learn about religious life from him?

DSR: I had the great good fortune to know Bede Griffiths for a long time.[6] We first met in the early 1950s when he visited our community at Mount Saviour, and we stayed in touch until he died in 1993. I greatly admired Father Bede for how he managed to integrate Indian and Christian religious sensibilities. He celebrated Mass at Shantivanam with the reverence and beauty of a *puja* in a Hindu temple. In a truly creative way, he adopted elements of Hindu worship into the Christian liturgy. I will always remember the climactic moment when, to the sound of bells, he was wafting a camphor fire around the Eucharistic gifts of bread and wine. A liturgical celebration with Father Bede was an unforgettable experience. The enculturation of the Christian liturgy into Indian culture became his lasting accomplishment. Church authorities did not make this easy for him, but he persevered.

JK: He did understand the importance of Christian enculturation.

DSR: Yes, in the truest sense of the word. He was deeply convinced that all religions breathe one spirit. And that spirit was alive in him. He kept his eyes on the Mystery that is alive in all religions and unites them. He was so enthusiastic for that unity, and so intellectually convinced of it as well, that expressing it in the liturgy and in his own way of life was completely natural. He wore the saffron robes of the sadhus, the Indian monks. Attempts at enculturation by adopting one or another little detail can be artificial and contrived, but with Father Bede, everything was organic and fitting.

JK: You asked whether all traveling might be triggered by a sort of homesickness. Normally, we feel as though it is a longing for distant travel—wanderlust—that drives us. What do we seek when we set out into the world?

DSR: Wanderlust and homesickness are not all that different. Sometimes I am not at all sure whether one or the other is driving me. In the end, a barely conscious longing to venture deep into the Great Mystery may express itself in both our inward quest and in our outward journeys. Our most important journeys in life do not need to be long or lead us to faraway places. Walking over to the next village may turn out to be more of an adventure journey than my traveling around the world by plane. What matters is the attitude—openness for encounters, courage to expose oneself to surprise.

JK: One undertakes something, be it out of homesickness or wanderlust. One moves, one changes. Staying in place will not do. We humans evidently need to journey—either inward or outward, in some way, shape, or form.

DSR: To live is to change. And change is the essence of journeying.

JK: *Homo viator*—man is a wanderer.

DSR: In one of his prayers, Rilke says to God, "When I go toward you, it is with my whole life."[7] The movement of our lives is a journey in this sense, a journey home, if you will.

JK: But the journey home also requires detours, ways out, and sometimes ways of escape even, to become truly a journey home. Since you are familiar with the religious situation in many parts of the world, your assessment of it interests me. Because religion is a worldwide phenomenon, if, for example, you compare Europe with the United States, the former seems to be far more atheist than the latter. In the United States, an open and vocal commitment to religious faith and invoking religion to justify one's positions and actions is almost normal, while in Europe, about 42 percent of people see themselves as atheist or close to atheism—including many of those baptized as Christians. Nietzsche's statement that God is dead, which we have already alluded to, seems to prove true in practice. In our public spaces in Europe, an existential-practical atheism or a complete indifference to religion—an apathy—has become the rule rather than the exception. Often, being religious or believing in God is seen in one's circle of friends as a little strange, if not downright suspicious. How do you understand this? How do you interpret this mood, which may be rather unique to Europe in comparison with the rest of the world?

DSR: In the United States, we encounter a very widespread fundamentalism, and I personally do not like its rhetoric, its God-talk. I regret that, in Europe, so many Christians are leaving the Church. It may represent a necessary inner liberation for those leaving, but it also means a loss for their children, because then the next generation no longer experiences religious belonging. The sense of security provided by religious embedding is important in childhood, even if one leaves that safe shelter later. Children need it and enjoy it as well. But in the end, the heart of religiousness is engagement with Mystery, and no one can avoid that forever. The birth of a child; the death of one's parents, friends, or relatives; one's own death—all these are situations that are deeply religious because they confront us inevitably with the Mystery of life and challenge us to somehow interact with it. In our society, people often try to invent some ritual on those occasions. What a great gift it is to grow up in a culture where tradition gives one forms to express the religious dimension in everyday life, where people inherit rituals for that, as in the indigenous cultures. How that enriches human life!

JK: No doubt, but even your interpretation of birth and death as experiences of the Mystery, as religious experiences, would be completely denied by a "religiously unmusical" agnostic. He might say, "Brother David, birth is birth, death is death. That's the circle of life, it has nothing to do with God or Mystery. We pass life on and it is over when we die. Our highest goal in life is to pass life on to the next generation in such a way that they treat the world well. That is why it is important that the next generation live relatively decently and think well of us. We gave them life, but there is nothing beyond that."

DSR: Someone who strikes such an "it's nothing but" pose is not really engaging with life. Imagine a woman who would say what you have just said: "Birth is birth." When she gives birth to a child, she surely will be overawed—and the father who witnesses the birth as well. Or when one is standing at the deathbed of a person one loves: that is engaging with life, and there, all formulas break down—the religious ones no less than the atheist ones. What remains is experiencing, and that experiencing is the experiencing of the Holy, of a power that both thrills us and makes us tremble. That's what religiousness is all about.

JK: But not for those who do not see it.

DSR: I do not know whether there really are people who do not see that. There may be those who deny it, but is there someone who really does not experience it?

JK: Perhaps not experiencing it as wonderful, but in the sense of a profane finite life. It is always wonderful when new life comes into the world and sad when a life passes.

DSR: Presented that way, all it means is that someone does not think overly much about the Mystery of life. But that is not what matters in the end: it only matters not to actively deny it. And one can deny it with the head, but not with the heart. That, at least, is how I see it.

JK: But does one experience the religious or the Holy itself, or is experiencing already an interpretation?

DSR: Naming it is of course an interpretation, but what stands behind that interpretation is lived reality. One may call it whatever one pleases.

JK: Do you not know people who essentially say, "There is no God. Life is beautiful. Let's drink and eat, because we'll be dead tomorrow"?

DSR: I do not know many such people, because my social contacts are limited. But a person's stated doctrine is irrelevant in our context here. In other words, when someone says, "There is no God," I try to look at the person standing behind this statement. That is the same when I encounter a fundamentalist. I try to encounter the person. The doctrine does not interest me so much. We can pretend all sorts of things to ourselves.

JK: Then what is the essential factor?

DSR: In the end, what counts is that we let oneself be moved by Mystery, not the terms we use to talk about it—and that is also true for people who use Christian terms. If the Mystery has not taken hold of us, reciting this or that creed is no substitute. Fortunately, life runs its course in such a way that encounters with the Great Mystery are unavoidable. At the very least, we encounter death. Death confronts us with something we cannot grasp but that we must deal with when it takes hold of us. The same holds for music or nature. I am convinced that music and nature trigger the relevant religious experiences in many people. When the Mystery takes hold of us, it takes us into the space that Rilke calls "the world's inner space." And that is what counts, not interpretive terminology.

JK: A brief question about "the world's inner space": What exactly is meant by that?

DSR: Rilke used different expressions for this reality: "the world's inner space," "the open," "the inaccessible." Those are poetic terms, and one needs to allow oneself to be affected by them. Something resonates in us there, but grasping it, analyzing it, and putting it into the harness of logic, that is impossible. In the end, it comes back to being moved.

JK: And about mutual belonging?

DSR: Being moved by the Great Mystery is the experience of boundless mutual belonging. Of course, one can cultivate one's consciousness of this belonging and let it flow into one's whole life. But one can also repress it.

JK: And what can you do for someone who suppresses and denies it?

DSR: I would start by giving that person a big hug. There is more genuine religiosity in a heart-to-heart hug than in all the God-talk in the world. Where strangers learn to hug one another as friends, the Mystery shines forth in all its glory. Is not the longing for encounters of this kind the deepest reason for our travels?

Traveling with Anthony Chavez

8

CONTEMPLATION AND REVOLUTION

1996–2006

The more I encountered people from many parts of the globe on my travels and the more I listened to their concerns, the more I began to suspect that a sea change in the history of the world was approaching. All the most memorable encounters centered around tears, but also around inextinguishable hope. Especially one conversation—with students in Zaire—triggered insights that would crystallize and become decisive during the eighth decade of my life.

I am in Kinshasa. The unrest here has reached a point where each night I must be brought to new, less endangered quarters. One evening, I visit doctoral students in their rundown dormitories, where they live cramped into tiny spaces with their wives and children. The only table they have is a cooking surface, dining table, children's play area, and desk all-in-one, so that the expensive books and the documents for their dissertations are constantly in danger. Despite unimaginable deprivations, these young men have managed to get near the goal of all efforts. "What is the thing you most hope for in your future?" I ask them, thinking—admittedly—of riches and influence. The answer makes me speechless. "Once we have finished, we hope to resist the temptation to howl with the pack. We want to do it differently from those who have money and power now. We know, this will not be an easy road, but we'll try." Here is a radical new vision of the future. The courage of these pioneers to swim against the stream goes to my heart and shatters my preconceived notions. Their vision is—in the best sense—revolutionary.

Over time, *revolution* becomes an important term for me. I use it half-jokingly, since it concerns something quite different from the revolutions we know from history. The revolution that this moment in world history demands of us must revolutionize even the accepted image of revolution. Until now, revolution has consisted of turning the respective power pyramid on its head, so that the former revolutionaries climbed from the bottom to the top—and continued doing what those on top had done before. Today, it is not enough to turn the power pyramid upside down; we must completely dismantle and replace it by a network. The Buddha made it his goal to put this into practice in the social structure of his *sangha*,[1] and Jesus wanted to see it realized in his community of disciples: "The kings of the Gentiles lord it over them; and those in authority over them are called benefactors. But not so with you; rather the greatest among you must become like the youngest, and the leader like one who serves" (Luke 22:25–26). The doctoral students in Kinshasa obviously wanted something similar. Their vision and goal, like that of many other small groups I was privileged to encounter, was not an improved power hierarchy but rather a network of mutual respect.

From the beginning, the pyramid has been the fundamental model of our civilization. Most people have accepted and continue to accept that model as a given. But without a clear picture in their minds, they simultaneously desire something completely different. People blossom under mutual trust, but our creativity dries up under fear. The power pyramid is built on fear: those at the top fear losing their power and, therefore, use violence to maintain their place. Further down in the pyramid, fear leads to rivalry and cut-throat competition. The fear of losing out leads to greed, jealousy, and envy. In a network, in contrast, there is no position of power to defend, because all are empowered to work for the good of all others. This revolutionary vision of the future replaces fear by trust, rivalry by cooperation, greed by communal sharing.

History was never my favorite subject. Under Hitler, we were convinced that our history professors were lying to us, because all the past had to be tailored toward its glorious culmination in the Third Reich. But now I wanted to examine the fundamental idea behind the French Revolution. Although the movement soon turned completely in the wrong direction, I found its original premise fascinating: "*Liberté, Égalité, Fraternité*"—did that not contain the program for the fresh start that was urgently needed even then but might today be necessary for our survival?

Freedom (*Liberté*) begins and ends with freedom from violence, to which I have sworn myself. Violence makes one unfree, since it is the perversion of power. The only creative use of power is the empowerment of others, and it frees the one who empowers no less than the one who knows himself empowered.

Equality (*Égalité*) does not mean raising everyone to the same level, but rather ensuring equal rights and equal dignity. It became increasingly clear to me that a dynamic order can only be built on the acknowledgment of our equality. Where we conquer fear, competition turns into interplay of give and take among people with quite different talents, but with equal rights—and equal responsibility.

Fraternity (*Fraternité*) puts a new emphasis on equality by naming its origin: as brothers and sisters, we all are part of the same human family. Thus, fraternity points also to the most beautiful expression of being a family: sharing.

More than ever before, in my seventies, I also had the opportunity of meeting people who stood at the helms of our society in the United States and elsewhere, and whom I could therefore presume to be well informed. Again and again, I heard particularly these people speak the words, "We can't go on like this!"—not in politics, not in economics, and not in any other significant area either. "And why not?" I would ask. "Because we are in the process of destroying ourselves." (And, at that time, there were still many more who thoughtlessly exploited nature and the environment, calling climate change a hoax while still considering themselves experts.) Through violence, rivalry, and greed, we now stood near the brink of self-destruction; and in the thirty years since, we have come significantly closer. But during the same period, ever more people have woken up to the realization that our hope in the future lies in sharing, cooperation, and freedom from fear and violence.

Power pyramid and network proved to be helpful models for understanding my personal experience in this period of my life. At its beginning (1994–97), I was teacher-in-residence at Esalen Institute on the Big Sur coast of California, close to the New Camaldoli Hermitage, my monastic home for fourteen years, as noted earlier. Archaeological finds have shown that even five thousand years ago, Native Americans of the Esselen tribe and their ancestors had their winter grounds near the hot springs at this place that nature endowed so richly. In the early 1960s, many young people settled by these hot springs, living in a counterculture style and questioning the prevailing social order. The spark that kindled Esalen's future was their idea to invite intellectual pioneers of the time as teachers and guides: Abraham Maslow, Joan Baez, Paul Tillich, Henry Miller, Fritz Perls, Timothy Leary, Carl Rogers—even a cursory and incomplete listing is impressive. Hot springs by a steep cliff face above the thundering bay; bathing pools overlooking the sea and the playgrounds of whales, dolphins, and sea otters: all that was seductive enough to attract even the most prominent of guests without a speaking fee. Soon, the retreat developed into a nonprofit center for interdisciplinary humanistic studies and conventions. The resident community carried the life of the center, while its owners and a board of directors managed it as a business.

Perhaps equally important was the fact that the massage technique that developed there soon grew in fame, and that gardeners coaxed not only indescribably glorious flowers from the fertile soil but also rich harvests of fresh vegetables, which inventive chefs turned into delicious vegetarian meals. Some of the women started a kindergarten to care for the children of the resident community. Soon guests too discovered that their little ones were well cared for at this progressively run Gazebo and enjoyed playing with the goats, dogs, and donkeys there while their parents attended courses or enjoyed the hot springs. Thus, the various talents among the resident community found rich expression and use, and the venture thrived.

Mike Murphy and Dick Price, both born in 1930, and later colleagues at Stanford University, incorporated Esalen Institute in 1961. Mike had inherited from his family most of this land where young people of the Beat generation were squatting. His grandfather, a doctor, had already considered making therapeutic use of the hot springs before there were roads leading to the Esalen wilderness. Both Mike and Dick lived at Esalen, but eventually Mike moved to San Francisco. As a disciple of Sri Aurobindo, he meditated with conviction and tenacity. He focused on his writing and felt responsible for the commercial unfolding of Esalen, which he furthered with the help of a supervisory board. Dick continued to live in the community and was connected to its members by mutual love and appreciation. Together with his wife, Chris, he was teacher, role model, inspiration, and communal center to the varied crowd who were doing pioneering work there. Having had bad personal experiences with psychiatric practices, he wanted to make Esalen a place of psychological healing, where inner processes could unfold organically and find balance. Using his own form of Gestalt therapy, he succeeded in giving Esalen its orientation as "a community of seekers serving seekers" that would make it a world-famous center of integral healing for body and soul.

On November 25, 1985, Dick was—as he did so often—meditating high in the hills near the spring supplying Esalen with water when he was hit by a falling rock and killed. (At the very same time, something moved me out of the blue to hold a speech of praise in his honor, even though I was over three thousand miles away and knew nothing of his death.) The passing of this man who had decisively shaped Esalen's inner life for more than twenty years was a blow that would forever change the direction of his and Mike Murphy's creation. Although Steve Donovan, the new director, was trusted by both the community and the supervisory board and did everything in his power to bridge the gap, the goals of the board and the community drifted further and further apart. Steve began to invite "teachers-in-residence": women and men who might encourage the community by their presence and charisma. I was one of those honored with an invitation. In one of those almost too dramatic scenarios of fate, the moment I arrived and put my suitcase down, Steve embraced me, picked up his suitcase, and left Esalen for good.

There I now stood, between the "village community"—as I viewed those who had come to Esalen in the early days with their families—and the "entrepreneurs," who saw it as their responsibility to turn Esalen into a profitable venture. On the one hand, women and men who had worked and lived there for much of their lives and even raised children there claimed an authorial right: Had they not made Esalen what it was? Did the guests not come because of the warm atmosphere of community that they had created and which could not live on in that way without them? On the other hand, the board was convinced that it had not only the right but the duty to transform the confusing welter of community into a well-organized staff. To this day, I do not know what lay in the realm of possibility at that time. With more patience and empathy, the tensions might have been eased and the hurt of sudden, unexplained dismissals of honored long-time colleagues might have been avoided. But in the last analysis, what took place here was a clash of basic principles.

In retrospect, it seems that this was a demonstration of the conflict between network and power pyramid. While Esalen has done considerable service in programs for businesspeople—I myself was privileged to participate in several conferences at which entrepreneurs and groundbreaking pioneers in the field of economics introduced new, more humane models of leadership—Esalen's board still follows a conventional top-down administrative model. For now, the power pyramid has prevailed over the original network vision of Dick Price and the community. Their hopes for an egalitarian, cooperative, and humane business model are still waiting to be realized.

My time at Esalen was difficult for me, and my heart still grows heavy when I recall the suffering I witnessed. But I remain deeply thankful for the encounters and experiences that I received there. After my years in California, I returned to New York feeling that I had reached the end of my life. At that time, my friends Nancy and Roderich Graeff settled down in a Quaker retirement home not far from our monastery and offered to house me there as well. Father Martin, our Prior, familiar with the difficulties of caring for aging Brothers, gratefully accepted the offer on my behalf. And thus, Kendal at Ithaca became a new kind of hermitage for me that turned out to be exactly what I needed. I did not travel anymore, reduced all contact to a minimum, and prepared to die. Well, life was to unfold differently. Again, and again, Tom Driscoll and other friends urged me to put texts on the internet. They suggested gratefulness as a theme. I was not overly interested, but Daniel Uvanovic, an adventurous young internet expert whom I had gotten to know in Big Sur when he spent retreat time at the monastery, offered to come to Ithaca for a few weeks and build a website for me. The weeks turned into months and years, and Daniel most generously stayed on and worked tirelessly. From its humble beginnings, the website[2] grew to be a source of strength for a worldwide network of tens of thousands of visitors daily. In my heart, I gratefully carry the names—far too many to list here—of the friends and colleagues who made, and still make this work possible.

When we began, the Fetzer Institute gave us a starting grant and asked two questions to which we were supposed to find the answers: (1) Is the Internet suited to spirituality? and (2) Can one build a community on the Internet? Today, the answers have become so obvious that the questions sound like trick questions. The internet has enabled countless new forms of community and can be understood as potentially spiritual in and of itself. It can become the cyber-technical support structure for what Pierre Teilhard de Chardin called the noösphere—essentially a network of all-connecting love that spans and unites the world. Life is connection, and if spirituality is, by its very name, aliveness (the Latin *spiritus* means "breath of life"), then the cyber network is itself a spiritual phenomenon, since it leads to increased aliveness through connection.

The closer our website comes to its goal, the more revolutionary—and also contemplative—it will be. Our goal is it to provide online support for off-line groups of people the world over who support one another in living a grateful and, therefore, joyful life. Any such effort aimed at building a network of networks in our power pyramid society must be considered revolutionary. And to be revolutionary in the true sense, one must be contemplative.

It is a widespread misconception that contemplative must mean "turned away from the world." As early as my novitiate, I learned from Father Damasus how important the little syllable *con* is for understanding contemplative life. Just like the Latin *cum* (with), it indicates connection. The things that are to be connected in contemplation are an ideal image and its realization. Looking up at the sky shows us an eternal order, represented by the constellations, and this presentation is realized amid the world's chaos by the building of a temple. The syllable *temp* is ancient and originally means "measure." By looking up at the heavens, a contemplative person gains the measure by which the temple will be built on earth. That is why the earliest temples—such as Stonehenge—are something like giant sundials or star clocks. And in India, there is a saying: "When the temple's measurements are right, there is order in the world." As human beings, we are called to look up at the sky by our upright gait, and our free hands permit us to turn the ideal image into tangible reality: "on earth as it is in heaven."

In this way, work on the website becomes for me a new form of living contemplatively and of sharing this approach to life with untold numbers of people. This even turns out to be the beginning of that revolution to which I felt committed. Thus, to my surprise, at the threshold of a new millennium, my life continues and new opportunities arise.

DIALOGUE

JK: At first glance, mysticism and politics do not seem to fit together too well. We think of mysticism as a kind of interiority that is highly personal and thus not comprehensible or accessible to others. And politics, too, is often taken to mean merely the public exercise of power and its strategic preservation. You consider mysticism and politics together in your word pair of *contemplation* and *revolution*. Why is this impulse for social change so important to spirituality?

DSR: Understood correctly, spirituality means aliveness. The term comes from the Latin word *spiritus*, "life breath." Full aliveness means being awake to the responsibility we have in the face of the Great Mystery, but also to the responsibility we have in the face of the community, the *polis*, "politics." In this field, too, spirituality is an awakening. If we sleep through our responsibility to the public good, we are not truly spiritual. Not fully awake; not fully alive.

JK: As far back as Greek antiquity there was a distinction between the *polites*, those who were interested in and working toward the public good, and the *idiotes*, those who thought for themselves in private and were active only for their own prospects.

DSR: So, we do not want to be idiots.

JK: Regarding the revolutionary: In which spiritual tradition do you see yourself there? What role models are you thinking of?

DSR: Above all others, my role model is Jesus Christ as a revolutionary. He definitely was one and was recognized as such, in his time. Death by crucifixion was not a punishment for religious transgressions; those were punished by stoning. Crucifixion was an overtly political punishment, reserved for escaped slaves and revolutionaries—for transgressions by which the so-called criminal had undermined the existing social order. Jesus did that by inaugurating the kingdom of God on Earth. By saying, "The greatest among you ought to be the servant of all," he is undermining the power pyramid of his time—and of our time as well. Is that not decidedly revolutionary?

JK: What did he radically question at the time that we might still profit from today?

DSR: The abuse of power. In our surroundings, we all have more power than we realize: over our children, friends, colleagues, family, and so on. The only legitimate use of this power consists in empowering others. If we do not do this, then power turns to violence. Violence seeks to control, subjugate, exploit. That was the misuse of power Jesus turned against.

JK: Empower others, yes, but empower to what end?

DSR: Empower them to actualize themselves in community, to bring forth their best creatively.

JK: Living their full potential.

DSR: Their full potential. Precisely! What parents do for their children and teachers do for their students, if they are doing it right: drawing the best out of them.

JK: Can that also work in conditions of scarcity and crisis?

DSR: Crisis? Scarcity? The idea of scarcity is an interpretation arising from a lack of trust in life. We cannot allow ourselves this mistaken interpretation of the situation. If we live out of a consciousness of abundance, which is much more realistic than the idea of scarcity, we will also approach crises with a completely different attitude. Then the crisis is no longer the end of everything.

JK: And no longer without alternatives.

DSR: Correct! The word *crisis* comes from the same root word as *sieve*. *Crisis* means a process of "straining," of "winnowing out." In every crisis, all that is capable of life becomes separated from what is no longer capable of survival. There is a similar process in nature: when it pulls off the dried husks so that the young shoots can unfold freely.

JK: But one can also misinterpret that as Social Darwinism or misuse it for certain economic interpretations, such as, only those best adapted to the system survive—survival of the fittest. The strong then have the advantage over the weak because the latter have not had as much opportunity, are less well educated, or had the misfortune of being born in the wrong time, in the wrong place. Then fate, as it were, spits the weak onto the rubbish heap of history.

DSR: I do not want to deny that danger. But I would say yes, what is strongest survives—but—what is strongest is not violence but cooperation. Working together with others makes us stronger, that is, cooperation in service of the common good. Building one another up rather than keeping one another down. That is what I mean. The strongest are those who recognize that what makes us strong is that we orient ourselves in the direction of life, and life aims at cooperation, connection, networks.

JK: Coevolution?

DSR: Yes, coevolution. The strongest are those who are alert to coevolution and contribute to it. That is how things work. We can read this fundamental rule in nature and in history.

JK: In what do you read that, for example?

DSR: In the development of life. Without cooperation, living organisms could have never evolved this far. It is a misinterpretation to think that competition was the only force moving evolution forward. In that approach, we are forgetting about motherly love, for example. The supposedly strong would never have grown up if, at all advanced stages of evolution, there had not been the strong mother caring for her weak children. We forget that too easily.

JK: We also forget fatherly love.

DSR: It may be autobiographically typical that I am forgetting to mention that.

JK: It has its qualities too, of course. To return to your role models, you have already mentioned Jesus. Are there any contemporary role models as well?

DSR: Yes. I can immediately think of a woman: Dorothy Day. I visited her on my very first day in the United States, in 1947, and greatly admired her and the Catholic Worker Movement.[3]

JK: That is an organization that dedicates itself to those cast out by society.

DSR: Yes, and this organization is still extraordinarily alive and successful. It grew out of Dorothy's compassion for the poor and her struggle to overcome social injustice in the United States. Soon other communities grew out of the one she initially founded, in 1933, with Peter Maurin in New York City. Just like Mother Teresa, she cared for the poorest of the poor, but she went beyond that and questioned the social structure responsible for such poverty. That is why she spent years of her life in prison. Brazilian archbishop Hélder Câmara understood that when he said, "If I give food to the poor, I am called a Holy Man; if I ask why the poor are poor, I am called a Communist." Many Christian communities in Latin America also questioned the pyramid hierarchies of power based on their reading of the glad tidings of Jesus. Such approaches are often denounced as Communist.

JK: Correctly or incorrectly?

DSR: Correctly in the best sense of the term *communist*, meaning "strengthening community," but incorrectly in the sense of the international, political Communist movement.

JK: So, not in the sense of Communist party ideology.

DSR: Definitely not.

JK: In your pair of terms—*contemplation* and *revolution*—you redefined revolution as the dismantling of the hierarchical power pyramid and the rise of communities organized as networks. At first glance, that seems admirable, and I think I understand the kind of networks you have in mind. But to clarify, I will offer a critical counterargument, and as a devil's advocate, consciously misinterpret you. A subversive nongovernmental organization like the Mafia has recently also begun to organize as a network. Even terrorist organizations like the so-called Islamic State, with its streamlined, autonomously acting cells and network structures, have been highly successful in their attacks in Belgium, France, and Turkey. If a network has inward trust, that fact does not necessarily say anything about the ethics of that networked organization, only about its effectiveness. So, I am afraid that the new spirit you have in mind cannot be attributed solely to the form of organization.

DSR: No, not to the form of organization but to its use of power. The question is whether power is used to empower everyone in their uniqueness and interdependence. That is required. And it must apply to everyone. It must encompass all human beings, not merely a specific group.

JK: Meaning, the networks you are picturing have a universalist orientation?

DSR: Universalist and borne by respect for every individual person. But *respect* may be too pale a term. It is about deep care toward your neighbor, toward all other people, and toward life in all its forms. This great care, this reverence for life must be central.

JK: So, what Albert Schweitzer said: "I am life that wants to live, in the middle of life that wants to live."

DSR: Precisely that. That would be the spirituality of the networks I am referring to, and that fundamentally distinguishes them from those of the Mafia and the terrorists.

JK: You describe how in the 1990s, as a teacher at the legendary Esalen Institute in Big Sur, you had the opportunity of seeing these differing organizational structures—the pyramid and the network—firsthand, including their consequences. The community that had grown in and around Esalen wanted to live precisely this innovative, supportive, empowering network. In the end, however, a traditional model prevailed, with a board controlling the business. Is it possible that all-too-human motives worked more strongly there than an altruistic, cooperative spirit? Might these networks you are describing not also require, in some sense, reformed humans, or conditions for humans living and working together that are not a given in today's social system?

DSR: Yes, I think we need a new consciousness to accomplish the necessary change on a large scale. The prevailing structures and the established powers are still too strong. It takes great effort and courage for a pioneering vision to succeed. At Esalen, unfortunately the death of Dick Price meant the defeat of a more humane and egalitarian business model; his vision did not prevail.

JK: And why not?

DSR: The community's courage and moral strength were no match for the Board's power to fire those who stood up for Dick's vision.

JK: It probably also takes patience—it takes a long time to drill through thick boards—to stand the pressure that one might be exposed to for a long time.

DSR: Patience is definitely a virtue. But the exploiters will always tell you that you need to be more patient—to give them more time to exploit you. I am thinking of the medieval peasant uprisings that were put down in one bloodbath after another. They were demonized as outbreaks of impatience in our history books, because history is written by the winners. Those same books belittle all groups that, in the past, stood up for the power of love against the love of power.

JK: One can see the same thing when one looks at religious orders such as the Franciscans, who were quite revolutionary in the beginning. They were only able to survive because there was a humble pope at the time.

DSR: But in their original form, the Franciscans did not survive; the spirit of St. Francis was domesticated in their second generation. The Rule of their order was changed, and even the original stories were censored and altered. That makes me wonder: was destruction simply the end of all the promising beginnings in history that were nipped in the bud? Was there not something in them that cannot be destroyed? Did they not—for a moment at least—make something shine forth so genuine, so promising, so sublime that it must find completion—if not in time, then beyond time? I find consolation in Hölderlin's words: "What we are here, yonder, a God is able to complete."[4] I put this together with T. S. Eliot's deep intuition:

> "What might have been and what has been
> Point to one end, which is always present."[5]

The more I ponder these poetic insights, the more I come to trust that all positive efforts are somehow finding completion in a timeless realm. I cannot give any evidence of this, but the good, the true, the beautiful is, in its essence, not subject to time. All that we sacrifice for the true, the beautiful, and the good, all the effort we expend out of love, cannot be lost. What can I say? We need this conviction or else we would despair.

JK: The dominant model of thought propagated so successfully in the 1990s and still prevalent today is the idea of competition: we all are competing with one another, and that has been implemented even in the educational system. Advocates of this model argue that the competitive idea is ingrained in human nature; the goal is merely to steer it toward the good of society. One can see it in kindergarten, where children compete for the best toys and the teacher's affection; then in school, they compete for the best grades; at work, we compete for the best position, or the biggest paycheck; in art and culture, we compete for the highest degree of recognition; politicians compete for votes. Wherever we look, there is competition. But competition also means that there are winners and losers. Deep within us, we have come to believe that without competition, there would be no drive to expend effort and develop ourselves, to do something great. Therefore, it seems that competition and selection are important drivers of progress. Is that true, in your opinion?

DSR: Only to a degree. The idea of competition as we know it contains two aspects: the desire to excel, and the desire to outdo someone else. Those two are different, but so intertwined in our thinking that we can hardly tell the difference. Yet, it is a decisive difference.

JK: The difference might be between being good and being better than someone else.

DSR: Wanting to be good, wanting to surpass oneself is positive. But measuring how good I am based on how far down I can push someone else is not in harmony with life. We can see in nature what life intends. Here, every plant wants to realize itself and its full potential, not suppress the others.

JK: There are also weeds that will outgrow other plants and spread at the cost of the others.

DSR: But to understand the fact that plants spread at the cost of others as cutthroat competition would merely be an interpretation, and an anthropomorphism on top of that. Plants simply unfold, thereby influencing others and being influenced by them in turn.

JK: But in the plant world, there is also displacement. For example, several years ago, a plant from the Himalayas was introduced to the Alps and is crowding out endemic species on a massive scale simply because it is so much heartier. So, your image may not quite work.

DSR: Of course, I am all in favor of biodiversity. And the less we interfere with nature, the more its diversity thrives. But with plants, crowding out other plants is a by-product of their self-fulfillment, not its goal; that's the difference. When humans crowd each other out, they do it intentionally—and in the long run, it doesn't bring them fulfillment. We humans find our highest self-fulfillment through loving cooperation with others. I remember a report about Native American children who were given a soccer ball. They played with it enthusiastically, but as soon as they were divided into teams that had to play against one another, they lost interest. Their joy came from playing *with* each other, not *against* each other.

JK: I find that playing against each other has its charm as well, so long as it is a game and does not create shame or fear.

DSR: And as long as one can feel joy if the other wins.

JK: I play soccer with others, and I also want to shoot a goal myself. But when someone else from my team has that opportunity, I am overjoyed with him.

DSR: Can I not also feel joy when the other team scores a goal? Is it about winning against the opposite team, or is it about an exciting joint game? The better I play, the better I encourage others to play. That is competition as it is supposed to be, but unfortunately not as it is.

JK: Competition in quality, not competition for resources.

DSR: Yes, those are helpful concepts in dealing with this difficult subject. One aspect of competition at any rate, the effort to surpass oneself for the good of all, furthers a healthy development and should be viewed positively.

JK: The other idea of competition divides people into the successful—the winners—and the losers. We see that in the world at large: some economies are designed to leave others behind, and that has social consequences when competition leaves those other nations behind in their race for social and economic development. From the point of view of the system, that cannot be healthy.

DSR: The system is the important thing. One must look at the larger picture and see how the success of the individual affects that. In the larger framework, surpassing oneself should be seen positively, but self-actualization at the cost of others does not seem to support the system at large.

JK: Primarily because it comes from a wrong experience of the self. In the end, we are always from others, through others, and toward others.

DSR: Indeed! The wrong view of competition does come from an isolated, cutoff, and thus "sinful" I, from the Ego and not from the I-Self that knows itself connected with all others.

JK: Additionally, ever since Descartes, this Ego has been living in a bubble, imagining that it is only an I because it thinks. But thinking is only one possible self-description of a human being. By contrast, one might also say he "is" because he feels compassion, or is connected, or because he is at all—from the point of view of existence.

I was surprised that in the French Revolution's apparently secular program of *Liberté, Égalité Fraternité*, you see a program for new social order. You know that after the Revolution, thousands went to the guillotine in the name of these ideals. After the revolutionary impulse of liberation, a state terrorist regime followed, which was finally ended by another nationalist leader, in this case Napoleon, who tried to extend an imperialist reign over all of Europe. Why do you believe that with liberty, equality, and fraternity, we might have found a program for a new social order on which our lives may even depend?

DSR: Yes, of course, the French Revolution ended up completely antithetical to its origins. But the original ideal of liberty, equality, and fraternity—forgetting for a moment the historical derailments and looking only at the concepts themselves—is exactly what Jesus tried to realize. The truth will set you free (cf. John 8:32). You are all brothers. The greatest among you shall be the servant of all.

JK: So, you would see love for your neighbor as a brotherly love?

DSR: Yes, because we are all children of God.

JK: Today, liberty is enthusiastically advocated in the West but also elsewhere in the world. We want to be free and understand this freedom as very individual. But what we do not see enough is that there are societies that are captive; that is, that we also need liberation within society, not liberation of the individual for his or her own autonomous choices. The freedom of choice in our Western societies is very great. But liberty must be connected with justice and equality. We like to overlook that. I am thinking of a global justice, seeing the world as a system.

DSR: A just order implies both rights and duties. Of what we call justice today, the Romans said, "*Summum ius summa iniuria*" (extreme justice is extreme injustice). Justice as we see it in the criminal justice system, for example, is merely legalized revenge, as I see it. I was delighted to learn that, regarding criminal justice, the Argentinian constitution states (I'm paraphrasing): "Crime should not so much be punished as corrected and its repetition prevented." True justice belongs in a context of restitution and healing, not of revenge and punishment. In the case of a crime, that means—without excusing or minimizing it—helping criminals to become solid members of society again instead of locking them up or executing them.

JK: In Europe, we are currently experiencing the end of the economic growth model as we knew it even into the end of the 1990s. Our economies are no longer growing, or growing only insignificantly. At the same time, industrialized countries can no longer afford the road of expansive growth, purely for ecological reasons. If we want to realize the climate goals of limiting global warming to 1.5°C as set down by the United Nations in the 2015 Paris Agreement, that means that we need to quickly stop using fossil fuels and at least halve our use of resources, which would lead to a radical change in the Western lifestyle. If we do not manage that, we risk catastrophic climate events that will endanger our lives. We will see even greater wars and refugee movements than we do today, which is something we wish neither for ourselves nor our children. Pope Francis has recognized and stated this clearly in his encyclical *Laudato Si'*. Where do you see the duty of religion in these linked political, ecological, and economic questions? Does it have a duty there?

DSR: Yes, the very word *religion* points toward that duty. Related to Latin *re-ligare*, the word *religion* connotes a retying of broken bonds: bonds between us and our true selves; between us and all others; between us and the Great Mystery. Correcting our ecologically destructive activities is unquestionably a central aspect of mending our fractured relations to nature, to the world community, and to genuine humaneness. Pope Francis clearly understood this. As a voice in the wilderness, he keeps pointing out the connection between destruction of the environment and social destruction as its consequence. This is revolutionary and arises from his deeply contemplative insight.

JK: In this context, he used strong words: "Such an economy kills" (*Evangelii Gaudium* 53).

DSR: Yes! It is high time that religious representatives speak out in this regard.

JK: Not only speak out, but also live as role models within their institutions.

I was astonished that already in your early seventies, you were preparing for your eventual death. Not that it is completely unrealistic to engage with the idea of death, because we move toward death from our birth. But it surprised me how rationally you dealt with it. You moved to an old person's home in Ithaca, New York, which was made possible for you by good friends. But it evidently all turned out very differently. How did that happen?

DSR: What pulled me back out from my retirement was the creation of the website "Grateful Living." Initially, I did not regard this project as a task that would shape my future. It was just that friends recommended a website and insisted on the need for it. So, I gave in, and this website[6] turned out to be a small seed that suddenly burst forth and kept growing.

JK: You mean that it fell on such fertile ground that it now has versions all over the world?

DSR: No one could have foreseen that. But since I had some coresponsibility for creating this website, I wanted to do justice to that responsibility. That called me back out of my reclusiveness. My helping with the website made travels necessary. So, one thing led to another.

JK: This "Network for Grateful Living"—what is it, and what isn't it? Could you go into more detail about the fundamental reason behind it? What makes it so attractive and a possible alternative for people from completely different cultures and religious backgrounds?

DSR: Our Network for Grateful Living is a network of networks connecting people who have discovered the joy of living gratefully. From the very beginning, our website was conceived as a tool to support, all over the world, groups who are making an effort to live gratefully—small groups of people who help each other to live grateful lives, small networks that connect with one another. The website wants to provide online support for off-line action. Its phenomenal expansion showed us the power of this idea. Gratitude appeals to everyone. Thus, gratitude can connect people, and we are in urgent need today of ideas that connect. Gratitude can connect religions; every religion stresses gratitude as a high value. Gratitude can connect cultures; any child can understand it, and there is no culture that does not value gratitude; it is universally recognized. That is why today there seems to be a wave of gratitude spreading throughout the world, which is what we wanted to achieve—and I hope we contributed a bit. The idea has proved itself. Of course, questions arose: For what are we truly thankful? Can we be thankful for everything? And that led us to our next task for the site: to explain the concept of gratitude.

JK: How would you explain what gratitude is about and what it is not about?

DSR: Grateful living is an attempt to face life with trust, look for the opportunities life offers in each moment, and taste the joy of making the most of them.

JK: And why with gratitude?

DSR: Because the present moment, with all the possibilities it offers, is the greatest gift one can imagine. Everything there is can be understood as a gift to everything else there is. When we recognize that and live by it, we connect with all living things in each moment. That goes far beyond anything one imagines when one first hears the word *gratitude*. Unpacking its riches, exploring its meaning, and spreading the joy of gratitude is the goal of our website.

JK: Let me play devil's advocate once again; I can imagine someone saying, "Brother David is calling me to be grateful. So now I need to practice gratitude if I want to be a good guy. It's suddenly another duty I am saddled with, another effort I must make. And besides, when I look at my life, I see so many things going wrong, so many things for which I cannot be grateful. With all my illnesses and other blows of fate, I'm lucky to have survived at all.

DSR: Or as someone quipped: I'm grateful for my bad luck; it is the only luck I've got!—But seriously: The most important keyword for grateful living is *opportunity*. Even the most challenging situations keep giving us opportunities for which we can be grateful: opportunities for learning to deal with adversities, for growing by dealing with difficulties, completely new opportunities for proving ourselves, and maybe even for creative protest. Those are gifts we did not wish for, but with a grateful attitude, we can recognize the opportunities they give us as gifts and use them creatively. A grateful life is a creative life because we learn to ask, "What opportunity does this present moment offer me?" By using that opportunity creatively, we show ourselves to be grateful.

JK: Even the fight for more justice in social conflicts—that too is a form of grateful living.

DSR: Definitely. I fully agree. We must not think about grateful living as if it were a private affair. Life means connectedness—in the end, limitless connectedness. That is why social responsibility is necessarily a part of grateful living.

JK: What you say about a grateful life sounds to me like a strategy for happiness.

DSR: Yes, our longing for happiness is the driving force behind grateful living. What we humans are looking for in the end is lasting happiness—happiness that does not depend on what happens. I call this type of happiness "joy," and joy even in the midst of unhappiness is a real possibility. We feel joy when we trust life, are in tune with life, give a full response to life—and that is what a grateful person does. Happiness has rightly been called slippery; it slithers away between your fingers. But the joy that springs from gratitude is solid; it remains the bedrock of life, even in our unhappiest moments.

JK: That means that I do not need to be happy first in order to be grateful.

DSR: On the contrary, I need to be grateful first, and that will make me happy.

JK: Why is that the case?

DSR: Because joy is identical to gratitude. If we give children some little gift and they get joy from it, we know that they are grateful, even if they do not say "thank you." By saying "thank you," they show that they are well socialized; that's something different. But true gratitude is joy. That holds true also of gratitude in adults. Living with joy means living gratefully, and living gratefully means living joyfully.

STOP THE
CYCLE OF
VIOLENCE

Peace demonstration with Zentatsu Richard Baker Roshi (center) and Thich Nhat Hanh (center-right); New York, June 12, 1982

9

DOUBLE REALM

2006–2016

As a young man on one of my first visits to New York City, I strolled up Fifth Avenue one evening and, at 59th Street, wandered into the southeast corner of Central Park. In the early 1950s, this corner of the park housed a small zoo. Most of the zoo's regular visitors were children, and at this late hour, I was there alone. But suddenly, I felt a powerful presence, looked up, and saw a gorilla sitting on the roof of his hut. His massive form seemed to tower hugely in the dusk, and yet he was sitting there hunched over, as if grieving. As I approached, I could see into his eyes, but it seemed that he hardly noticed me, as if his thoughts were somewhere far away. He was old, maybe very old. I cannot say how long we stayed like that, holding each other's gaze, but I know that it was a long time. Long enough to tell me something about aging, an intuition deep enough that I still have not fully plumbed it, not even in the last decade of my life so far—I say "so far" because I have learned to expect surprises, and because there do remain mysteries that wait to be plumbed.

In this stage of my life, my inner plumb line tends to sink into depths that I can best explore with the help of Rilke's term "double realm." The poet writes,

And though the pool's reflection
often blurs before us:
Know the image.

Only in the double realm
do the voices become
eternal and mild.[1]

The double realm is one indivisible whole, though my thinking keeps wanting to pull its two aspects apart. Distinguish—yes! Separate—no. Looking at the world with eyes that try to encompass the whole, not permitting it to fall apart in my mind, I see that as my great task in aging. T. S. Eliot knows the difficulty of this task:

Let me disclose the gifts reserved for age
To set a crown upon your lifetime's effort...
As body and soul begin to fall asunder.[2]

On some days, it really does seem as though everything were about to fall asunder: I accidentally drop my spelt roll into a plate of pumpkin soup with corn oil and splatter my white robe from head to toe in yellow and black—the Austro-Hungarian Empire's Imperial colors. Is this my "second childhood"? In my first childhood, my mother told me that the first time she put a plate of spinach soup in front of me on the table, I got so excited about its beautiful color that I put both hands into it and painted myself green from top to bottom. Mother laughed, as she told me about it, and now the Brothers laugh kindly at my little accident in the refectory and suggest, "Perhaps one could call it 'art in action!'" That is at least a more positive interpretation than that all is falling asunder.

But what is it that suggests the image of body and soul falling apart in aging and death? I try to find an answer: I am aware that, on the one hand, my soul, my Self, lives in the Now and is thus not bound by time, while my body, on the other hand, has a beginning and is moving toward my daily approaching end. So, in my body, I am tied to time, and my I is ephemeral, while my Self has permanence. And yet I experience myself as a unit, as I *myself*—not as *I* and *self*. However, I am aware of this unity only as long as I live in the Now, in the moment, in the double realm of time and eternity. As soon as I hold on to the past or become entangled in fantasies of the future, I am aware only of the passage of time and the fact that my time is slipping away. ("I'm slipping, I'm slipping away, like sand slipping through fingers," says the poet.)[3] All the more, I consider it my great task to recognize that time and eternity do not lie next to each other but are one in the Now. My challenge is to live in the dynamic tension of the double realm.

While I am traveling, I have no choice but to meet that challenge; I can't afford distraction; can't manage unless I live in the Now. And what a gift it is that I am still able to travel. In fact, in the ninth decade of my life, I traveled more often, more extensively, and with lots more fun than ever before. This was due to the fact that now I no longer traveled alone. Since I can no longer hear the announcements in airports, need glasses to read the signs (but where are they when I need them?), and find that scanning electronic boarding passes is for a younger generation, I kept my eyes open for a young travel companion and found Anthony Chavez. He had just earned his college degree, was ready to take some time off, and proved willing to help me.

It became an immense joy for me, in the late autumn of my life, to show a youngster "the wide world"—Paris, Rome, Sydney, Moscow, Mumbai, Buenos Aires, Shanghai, London, Hong Kong, Istanbul, Vienna (I could double and triple that list). No less work now, but lots more fun. We went to see the Mona Lisa and the Sistine Chapel, walked the labyrinth at Chartres, rode elephants in Thailand and camels in the Sahara, and on all those travels,

"Monkey" kept us company. This mascot of ours was a thumb-size toy monkey who seemed to enjoy posing for photographs with the Eiffel Tower, Niagara Falls, the Blue Mosque, or Red Square as background. He traveled on Anthony's lapel and, during our audience with Benedict XVI, the Pope's bewildered glance went back and forth between Monkey and the Mohawk haircut that Anthony was sporting at the time. My young friend's spirit and energy rejuvenated me: he got this old geezer to paddle a kayak in Alaska, climb the campanile in Florence, learn to surf on a boogie board, and go zip-lining on Kauai. But the best in all this was that we encouraged one another in the practice of returning again and again to the Now.

For seven years we traveled together, and although it was, admittedly, not always smooth sailing, it gave me great pleasure to see Anthony thrive and mature. He was justly proud of his grandfather, Cesar Chavez, the great labor leader and civil rights hero, but he was quite able to stand on his own legs. In the end, I felt as proud as if I myself were his grandfather when Anthony worked his way to a position with *The Education Trust—West* that gives a wide scope to the best of his talents: compassion, a bright mind, and a keen sense for fairness.

Without a companion now, my travels took on a new form, but they did not become fewer and they did not become shorter. On the contrary, I was welcomed on a continent still largely new to me—South America. New friends, Alberto and Lizzie Rizzo from Buenos Aires, enthusiastic about gratitude, worked with amazing dedication at sharing the joy of grateful living with hundreds of thousands, just as my friends Peter Kessler, Brigitte Kwizda-Gredler, and Mirjam Luthe-Alves had begun to do in Europe. To my great joy, new websites of the Network for Grateful Living sprang up; now the message went out no longer in English only, but in German and Spanish as well. Now, workshops, seminars, and practice groups developed through the enthusiasm, devotion, and effort of volunteers on three continents.

In Argentina, I felt received and surrounded by such a warm outpouring of maternal energy that I now revere the maternal aspect of the Great Mystery under a new image: even before I was born, my parents had placed me under the protection of the "Magna Mater Austriae," Our Lady of Maria Zell, and I wore a medal with her image on a chain around my neck; later, my favorite image became that of the Virgin of Guadalupe; now I also love the image of Nuestra Señora de Luján. I entrust myself to her protection when flying back to Argentina, whether to shoot a film in Patagonia, engage in a dialogue with Father Anselm Grün before a thousand readers at the Buenos Aires book fair, or simply to admire the beauty and power of the waterfalls of Iguazú. Yes, in my old age, friends have added the gift of such "pleasure trips" to my schedule. In this new phase of traveling, I let myself be placed on a direct flight and be picked up at the airport of my destination. That way, I can still manage it.

At the same time, I keep making journeys inward to new regions of the double realm. Since the double realm is undivided and indivisibly one, I do not have to leave the "surface" behind to journey into its depths. On the contrary, eternity appears in the midst of time and space—shines forth and throws light on my path. All that lies behind me on this path was necessary to bring me to the place where I am now, and everything that lies ahead can be reached only from this present vantage point. Rilke helps me name what lies before me, waiting to be discovered: "the world's inner space," "the open," "the nameless," and finally "the inaccessible"—the Mystery. This no-thing is immense and simple. All else, by contrast, seems incomprehensibly multitudinous, an inextricable tangle of connections.

Much more often than before, I think about my ancestors and try to imagine them, far back. A past I'll never come to know has written the script for my life. My right palm exhibits a contracture that does not bother me, but reminds me that I might have inherited it from Viking ancestors.[4] What raids and rapes might lie in my past, or what pogroms, in which my noble Polish ancestors might have massacred my Hasidic Jewish forebears. How did these disparate strands flow together into one person? The word *person* comes from the Latin, *persona*, and used to mean "the role, the mask through which an actor's voice sounded." What past events might have fashioned the mask my Self is wearing now, and shaped the role I play today? Yes, the metaphor of role-playing seems fitting for this double realm of my *I* in the river of time and my *Self* beyond time.

On the first Sunday of each month, the monks at Gut Aich monastery put on a puppet show after the children's service. One and the same Brother can play two characters: say, the princess, with one hand, and the crocodile with the other. In the same way, the one grand Self can play countless roles as well. When I meet a crocodile, it helps to remember that the One whose hand is inside that monster upholds me from within with her other hand. My Self, which is at home in the Great Self, thus plays the role assigned to me. In playing, *Self* and *I* become one; I can distinguish between them but never separate them.

I ask myself what it means to play my role "well." The answer must be that playing the role well means playing with love—expressing, by the very way we live, a joyful yes to limitless belonging. If the I denies this yes, the Self nevertheless gives it the strength to play on, but the I—it now has become the Ego—is playing its role poorly. Only love knows how to act.

"Only through love is anything beautiful! Only through love is anything good!"[5] But what if the Self—to retain the metaphor—takes off the hand puppet? What if the mask crumbles into dust? Is everything over, everything at an end? I would say that it is indeed at an end, but it is not over. I do not want to speak of a "life *after* death." If dying means that my time is at an end, then it makes no sense to speak of something "after." But even now, everything I experience has a dimension that transcends time and space. T. S. Eliot calls the Now "the moment in and out of time"[6]—it is in time and yet beyond time. In this double realm of the Now, time and eternity are one. Therefore, in eternity I cannot lose even the smallest detail of all that I hold dear in time. "All is always now," says T. S. Eliot—speaking a truth that cannot be denied. For, what is not now *is* not; it was or will be, and so, it has only a shadow reality in the past or future. But in the Now, time is gathered into eternity—and I have a share in this process. Rilke sees in this gathering activity our task in life, storing up our experiences: "We are the bees of the invisible, passionately gathering the nectar of the visible and storing it in the great golden honeycomb of the invisible."[7]

If this is so, need I feel anxious about dying? Well, I do feel anxiety. I admit it, but I do not need to fear. Anxiety and fear, though often confused, are not the same. We must clearly distinguish the two. Anxiety is unavoidable in life, but fear is optional. We are free to choose between fear and courage. Anxiety belongs to the life process, but fear is life-denying and destructive. The words *anxious*, *anguish*, and *anxiety* come from the Latin word *angustia*, meaning "narrowness, tightness." Our chest starts feeling tight when we get anxious; that's natural. It's natural also that we feel anxiety when life leads us through a narrow passage. But every tight spot challenges us to choose between fear and courage. Fear makes us refuse to go on, we buckle like a stubborn mule at a narrow gate and get stuck in anxiety. Courage doesn't rid us of anxiety, but trust in life gives us courage to pass through the tight spot. After all, we had to pass through a very narrow passage to be born into this world. Every time life makes us face another narrow spot, it offers us the opportunity for a new birth. I prove that to myself. I look back at the bottlenecks in my life—the tight spots—and see quite clearly: the more pressing the anxiety, the more wonderful the surprises that resulted from passing through. Reminding myself of that again and again gives me trust in life and even courage to die.

What also helps me when I think of dying is the role model of people whose death I have witnessed. Here, I recall two Brothers from Mount Saviour. The first is Brother Christopher, who oversaw the work of building the monastery. Though he was only forty, he had severe heart problems, and on this day, he was the reader during our midday meal. As server, I stood next to him when he began the reading: "But that same night the word of the LORD came to Nathan: Go and tell my servant David: Thus says the LORD: Are *you* the one to build me a house to live in?" Six verses later, he came to the passage: "Moreover the LORD declares to you that the LORD will make you a house" (2 Sam 7:4–5, 11; emphasis added). At that point, he quietly laid his head on the book and was dead.

A second encouraging example is the death of our Father James Kelly (we had to use his last name, as we had two Brothers named James). He went into the chapel one last time on the evening of Holy Saturday, saw how everything was set up for our Easter celebration, and whispered with the enthusiasm that was so typical of him: "I cannot wait for tomorrow!" Then he went to bed. In the morning, he was supposed to be cantor for the *Exsultet*, but it seems that he really could not wait and was now singing it in heaven.

About a week before my mother's death—she is already quite weak—Vanja Palmers, whom she loves like a son, comes to visit her from Switzerland. He tells her that today, on St. Martin's Day, there is a tradition at Sursee in Switzerland that children can earn pieces of cheese for pulling the most outrageous face. Though we do not set out cheese as our prize, we nevertheless all try to make more outrageous faces than the others. My mother, on her death bed, outdoes us all.

In his famous poem "Sailing to Byzantium," William Butler Yeats compares an old man to a decrepit scarecrow:

> ...unless
> Soul clap its hands and sing, and louder sing
> For every tatter in its mortal dress."[8]

I try to do that whenever something about my "mortal dress" has once again gone to tatters, and gratefully applaud all my limbs and organs that are still working. In that way, the things I can be grateful for increase every day. "My cup overflows" (Ps 23:5).

Daily this becomes clearer to me: gratitude is a celebration of love. Just as love is the lived yes of joyful mutual belonging, gratitude celebrates life with a joyful yes at every knot of the great network in which everything is connected to everything. As we live this yes with ever more conviction, love ripens ever more abundantly in the autumn sun of life. I now see it as my main task to simply allow this to happen, since "we do not die from death, but from fully ripened love."[9]

DIALOGUE

JK: Brother David, you began your description of the most recent decade of your life by relating an encounter you had with a gorilla in a zoo. That led you to reflect on the idea that we are essentially all living in a double realm: the I and the self, the profane and the holy, time and eternity. The question is how to unify these double realms, or rather how you, yourself, can manage to exist in these double realms without suffering from a kind of inner split.

DSR: There is just one double realm, not many. The antitheses you mentioned are different aspects of the one double realm. It is important to stress the oneness of the double realm. And those opposites do not polarize life; they are poles of an indivisible whole. Rilke coined the beautiful phrase "double realm"[10] to describe this wholeness we must never mentally divide.

JK: So, the practice consists of repeatedly putting oneself into or reimmersing oneself in what one might call this ontological realm, if I understand you correctly? That reminds me of the ontological difference between Being and beings.

DSR: We can avoid polarization by looking at one pole and already seeing the other pole within it. So, for example, I look at time and experience eternity in the Now that takes me beyond time. I look at a star and see a flower in the meadow of the night sky; I look at the flower and see the star in it. The entire cosmos is a double realm—the inner cosmos, too. I look at suffering and see in it the earthly face of love.

JK: You write that you are aware of oneness only if you live in the present moment, in the Now, in the double realm of time and eternity. When you hang on to the past or get entangled in fantasies of the future, your experience of time makes you anxious. It makes you aware of the shortness of life. That, in turn, can spark fear, fear of death. What is it that causes your anxiety?

DSR: There are two things that make me personally anxious when I think of dying. First, there is the fact that we do not know what awaits us in death. We simply do not know. We are walking toward something that is not only unknown to us, but completely and utterly unimaginable. How can a caterpillar in a cocoon imagine what it is like to flutter from flower to flower as a butterfly? We too are walking toward something completely new. But things that are new and unknown make us anxious. Second, we know that dying is often connected to illness, suffering, and pain. That alone is enough to make me anxious when I picture it. Added to that, there is the prospect that today, sooner or later, one turns into nothing more than a case or a number in a hospital. This depersonalization makes me anxious as well. But quite apart from aging and dying, life is always scary in some way or another. What we need is courage.

JK: And what gives you courage, in this context?

DSR: In three syllables: trust in life. When I hit a tight spot, when my life's path gets narrow and I get anxious, trust in life becomes essential. My fear bristles against the anxiety—*I* puts out my bristles—and gets stuck in the anxiety. But my trust lets itself be carried forward and through. I know that I can trust life's power to carry me through like a swimmer trusting the buoyancy of water.

JK: You say that you do not want to speak of a life after death. Is there really that much room for misunderstanding?

DSR: Unfortunately, my refusal can easily be misunderstood; it may sound as though I were saying that death is simply the end. That is not at all what I want to say. What I mean is this: with death, my time is up, and when there is no more time, the word *after* has no meaning. I die when my time has run out, so how can I talk about something after? Time ends with death. My life ends on the level of time and space—I do not want to trivialize that. I want to confront it honestly; when I die, my space/time ends. But that does not mean that everything is over. Not at all! Even now, in the midst of time and space—in experiencing the Now—I can become aware of a dimension that is beyond time and space, and hence, death can make no difference to it.

Admittedly, I cannot avoid one difficulty: a person could say, "I have experience only through my senses, which are in time and space; I can think only with my brain, but when my brain turns to dust, what then?" In response, I can only say that here and now my senses and my thinking bring me to the border of something that is unbounded by space and time, is beyond space and time. And I belong to this dimension of my being—the Lasting—as much as I belong to time and space. That is exactly the double realm in which I live. This experience gives me trust and faith in something lasting, even when my bodily reality ends. Even now, I can touch a lasting reality. In the Now, I approach the Lasting. I need to be open to that, must feel my way into the Now, and learn to be at home there.

JK: No small number of Christians have trouble with the problem of a corporeal resurrection, because they think of it primarily as the resuscitation of a body. But we can see that the body disintegrates, reenters the big cycle of nature. That is the most obvious thing and needs no proof. But Christianity nevertheless claims a corporeal resurrection. What might that mean?

DSR: In order to answer your question, we must make sure we agree on what we mean when we say "resurrection." Most people think of it quite literally as the rising up again of someone who has died, a coming back. But that's the wrong direction. Correctly understood, resurrection does not mean coming back to this perishable life, but going forward into life in fullness, into life that lasts, into the Great Mystery. C. S. Lewis's novel *The Great Divorce* describes this movement "forward" beautifully.[11] The blessed in heaven ride toward an eternal sunrise, calling out to each other: "Higher up and deeper in!" The use of this image is well justified by early Christian tradition. It goes back—and maybe C. S. Lewis knew this—to the Cappadocian Fathers, who thought of resurrection-life as a dynamic journey of discovery into the Mystery of God.[12] Resurrection means that our "life is hidden with Christ in God" (Col 3:3)—hidden in the Great Mystery. When we try to understand "resurrection of the flesh," we ought to pay attention to the fact that "eternal life" is a reality with which we are familiar even now; our life is both visible amid time and space and hidden in the Now that transcends time and space. In the double realm, all my experiences partake of a visible and an invisible reality. So, when the visible ends, the invisible perdures—as it does even now, when we remember the past.

JK: But memory is a phenomenon of time.

DSR: Memory is a phenomenon *in* time, but only a reductionist would insist that memory is *only* in time. Yes, there are things such as neural constellations, records of some kind that are accessed when we remember; that can be shown experimentally. But there is more to memory. Remembering is more than recording plus reproducing. Any tape recorder can accomplish that. Human memory belongs to the double realm and partakes of the world's "outer" as well as "the world's inner space," as Rilke calls it. He turns that insight into the poetic image that we are the "bees of the invisible." All life long, we are harvesting our experiences into the "great golden hive of the invisible"[13]—into the world's inner space. There, nothing can ever be lost. And what I have stored there is my unique contribution. We are so different from each other that no two people can look at, let's say, a rose and see the same thing. With my unique sensibility, I enrich the interior world. I enrich it over the course of my entire life, not just with my pleasant experiences, but with all my pain and my tears as well. Everything is worthy to last.

JK: We hope that suffering, too, will be transformed. So, let me ask again in a different way. Is transience transformed as well?

DSR: It is being transformed even now. Now or never. The fifteenth-century mystic poet, Kabir, asks, "If you as a living being do not break your chains, shall spirits do so when you are dead?" He bluntly insists that to expect "eternal blessedness, simply because one is being eaten by worms," is wishful thinking. What you find now you will have found then, what you neglect now you will have neglected then. You must receive and embrace the Great Guest here and now.

JK: I need to dig a little deeper there. If I am understanding you correctly, intransience means being removed from the temporal stream of transience. In some sense, we cannot think of it any other way, being bodily creatures. It is obvious that the body changes even during our lifetime. But I am thinking of our form—we are always form and thus recognizable. If I am lucky enough, Brother David, I would like to meet you again in heaven at the "honeycomb"—and be able to recognize you.

DSR: Even now, it is the case that after twenty years, we have no difficulty in recognizing old acquaintances, and yet no cell in their body remains the same. What we recognize is the form. And "form of the body" is the definition of the *soul*.

JK: *Anima forma corporis est*, as scholastic theologians have said. "Soul is the form of the body."[14]

DSR: *Soul* means "that which makes this body this body"—and not just the body, but what makes this person this unique person.

JK: The soul is our unique aliveness.

DSR: Because we live in the double realm, we all have double citizenship, as it were: I am alive in time and space, but also in a greater Self beyond time and space.

JK: Brother David, I cannot help noticing how intensely your life's path is accompanied by art: its beginnings in visual arts, but also by music and especially by literature and poetry. Clearly, you admire Rilke, Eichendorff, Morgenstern, Trakl, Celan, Stifter. In Germany, the North American poets—David White, T. S. Eliot, e.e. cummings—are less well known. The last of these has a special significance for you.[15]

DSR: Cummings's poetry has grown very dear to me: it is very close to my heart. The quote of his that is most important to me is "i am through you so i." It is the climactic last line of a love poem that simultaneously has overtones of a prayer, just like Rilke's "Extinguish My Eyes" was a love poem and was then inserted into the *Book of Hours* as a prayer.[16] Our deepest personal encounters in life always resonate with the Great Mystery. I could not express my own lifelong relationship with the Divine Mystery any more fittingly than in the sentence "i am through you so i." What makes us persons is the richness and depth of our relationships. One's being a person deepens and matures through each new encounter. In every deep human encounter, we can say: you make me be what I am. But in our encounter with the Great Mystery, we realize an even deeper truth: that we can say "I" only because we stand face to face with a primordial You.

Ferdinand Ebner and Martin Buber each in their own way demonstrated what "i am through you so i" means: beyond each human You, we are in relation to a mysterious You, mysterious in the sense that the Mystery, itself, is our ultimate You.

I remember how in my early years as a monk, I would wander over the hills around the monastery, simply praying the word *You*, over and over. The same is told of a great Hasidic master; he prayed, "You, you, you!" Is that not prayer enough?

JK: It reminds one of the Prayer of the Heart.

DSR: Yes, indeed. The Prayer of the Heart is also a prayer to the You, in the end. The older I become, the more important this "i am through you so i" becomes for me. When our I passes out of space and time, our relationship with the primeval You remains. That was and is the fundamental First from which everything comes, and it will be the Last that remains. And for me, this sentence of "i am through you so i" belongs in a context with Rilke's stanza:

> When I go toward you
> it is with my whole life.
> [For who am I and who are you
> if we do not understand each other?][17]

Taken together, these two poetic insights give me more orientation and direction in life than any philosophical and theological discourses.

JK: Because they come closest to the essence of the phenomenon, one could say?

DSR: Yes, one can put it like that. Poetry goes to the heart of the matter.

JK: Brother David, I have no idea yet what it feels like to be ninety years old. I'm sure I'll have to face things that I can't even imagine yet, when I myself get there. But I am not the only one who admires how awake, curious, alive you still are at your age.

DSR: What helped me most in this respect was my contact with young people. Especially my travels with Anthony Chavez kept me—to use your terms—*awake*, *curious*, and *alive*.

Before Anthony joined me, I used to travel from one speaking engagement straight to the next. But with Anthony, we squeezed in little side trips, just for fun. Anthony got smarter and smarter at making cheap travel arrangements so we could afford little detours. He took me to places I had missed in all these years, although I had been near them: Yosemite, the Grand Canyon, and Uluru, the sacred Rock in the heart of Australia. We attended a performance of *Swan Lake* in St. Petersburg, explored Kangaroo Island together, and celebrated Anthony's birthday on the Great Wall of China. One special pleasure was reading books together—Pushkin on a river cruise in Russia, Adam Smith in his hometown, while waiting my turn for a TED talk at Edinburgh.

JK: You said it was fun. It must have also been broadening for Anthony's horizon.

DSR: Especially through meeting teachers whom I admire and to whom I was able to introduce him; Fritjof Capra, Ramon Panikkar, Matthieu Ricard, and Tania Singer come to mind. Yes, and Eckhart Tolle, Lynne Twist, Chade-Meng Tan, David Whyte, and Ken Wilber—it would be a long list. Anthony's keen mind made the most of these encounters. He learned to memorize names and soon became my walking who's who for our connections. He knew when to hand me my glasses, even before

I noticed that I needed them. He wrote down in big letters on our iPad key words from audience questions I could not clearly hear, and discreetly showed them to me. He came to know my material so well that he'd produce poems or book excerpts at just the right moment without prompting. Anthony also showed that rare ability to come up with his own original ideas so that later we started presenting workshops together. Our favorite title was "Gratefulness at Over Eighty and Under Thirty." One aspect of gratefulness that we often explored together—living in the Now—has become my central concern.

JK: Is this what occupies, drives, moves you today in this possibly last full decade of your life?

DSR: Yes, more and more clearly, I see this as my great task: to live in the Now and to continue practicing being present in the Now. This has been my main task and simultaneously a great gift, being able to practice that for so many long decades. Perhaps our life is only prolonged because we have not yet learned to fully live in the Now.

JK: What gives you joy today—what still fills you with wonder and opens wide your heart?

DSR: To answer that question, I would need to list everything I encounter over the course of a day. Everything fills me with wonder, more so than ever. It starts when I open my eyes in the morning; the fact that I am given one more day, is that not a joyous surprise?

JK: I am still here...

DSR: Ah! I am still around! Everything, everything becomes worthy of wonder.

JK: Increasingly worthy of wonder, the older you become—how? After all, you could also say, "I am inured, I've seen this before."

DSR: On the last page of the last book of the Bible, the seer on the island of Patmos hears God say, "See, I am making all things new" (Rev 21:5). I think this promise refers not only to a great renewal at the end of history, but, above all, to life in the Now. We can learn to look at any humble thing and—overwhelmed by surprise—see it burst into being, at this very moment, in the morning freshness of a new beginning.

JK: Brother David, thank you for speaking with me.

DSR: I thank you for your questions.

NOTES

The title of this book, *i am through you so i*, is the last line of poem no. 49 in *50 Poems*, by e.e. cummings, which is both a love poem and a prayer. Cummings (1894–1962) spelled everything without capitals.

1. BECOMING HUMAN

1. I started walking at nine months, so I may have been three years old at the time of this memory.

2. My father had inherited the Café Siller in the Schönbrunner Allee from his uncle Franz Siller. The "Maria Theresa Palace" (*Maria Theresien Schlössl*) of the Café Meierei Siller, also called the "Marienvilla," was a handsome building with plasterwork ceilings, baroque fireplaces, and parquet flooring in star patterns.

3. Hans, born December 14, 1928, and Max, born thirteen months later on January 17, 1930.

4. Supposedly, *detta* is a Czech term of endearment meaning "auntie"—but in our case, it came from our early attempts to say *Schwester*, the German short form of "children's nurse." We loved our Detta—Elfriede Gödel. She came when I was approximately

three years old and stayed with us over more than twenty years, far into our adulthood.

5. IMI was a brand of detergent introduced by the Henkel company in 1929.

6. This dream became fundamental in that the image of merging with Christ fits as well with all subsequent phases of my becoming fully human. The dream did not, however, produce in me any feelings of awe or reverence. In fact, it was not emotional at all. Instead, I would say that it sparked an insight in me that was far beyond my comprehension at the time but stayed in my memory as significant for perhaps that very reason.

7. Molybdomancy became a common New Year tradition in the Nordic countries and Germany, Switzerland, and Austria. Classically, tin is melted on a stove and poured into a bucket of cold water. The resulting shape is either directly interpreted as an omen for the future, or it is rotated in candlelight to create shadows, whose shapes are then interpreted.

8. Plato, *Theaetetus*, trans. Benjamin Jowett (Teddington: Echo Library, 2006), 155d: "This feeling of wonder shows that you are a philosopher, since wonder is the only beginning of philosophy."

9. Theodor Haecker (1879–1945) was a German writer, cultural critic, and translator. He was among Catholic existentialism's most eloquent defenders and one of the most radical cultural critics of the Weimar Republic and the Third Reich.

10. Pius Parsch (1884–1954) was an Austrian Catholic priest whose writings contributed significantly to the liturgical movement. He was also highly interested in reevaluating the Bible with an eye to liturgical practice. As military curate on the Easter Front of the First World War, he encountered the liturgy of Orthodox Christian churches and decided to make the Bible a book for the people and liturgy comprehensible to all. After his return to Klosterneuburg Abbey, he held Scripture courses for the novices. From 1922 onward, he celebrated community masses in which

large parts of the Mass would be sung in German (the local language; these masses are commonly known as the *Betsingmesse*, or *Deutsche Singmesse*)—with the goal of encouraging more active participation by those hearing the Mass, as well as a return to early Christian service practices. His services are considered the origins of the liturgical movement in Austria.

2. BECOMING A CHRISTIAN

1. The Catholic youth movement Bund Neuland (Newland Union) was founded in 1921 as an offshoot of the *Christlichdeutscher Studentenbund*, or "Christian German Student Union." After the annexation of Austria in 1938, the Bund dissolved itself, but was reestablished in 1948. In 1927, Anna Ehm and a group of young teachers from the Bund Neuland founded the *Neulandschule* (Newland School) in Grinzing, which was reopened in 1946; a new *Neulandschule* on the Laaer Berg followed in 1947. The pedagogical concept of the schools was based on holistic education in teaching and recreation, unhurried communication of knowledge, encouragement of community life, purposeful awakening of creative capacities, and Christian values as an orientation in life.

2. From Werner Bergengruen's *Poeta creator*: "Everything I created with you in mind, For your wellbeing; Then willingly accept the world, and with wakeful courage. Since as love created it even unto the poorest seedling—There is nothing that may frighten you, And you are at home."

3. The text of the song translates to "Thoughts are free / who may guess what they are? / They fly past / like shadows in the night. / No person can know them, / no hunter can shoot them. / The fact remains: / thoughts are free."

4. Ps 51:12: *Redde mihi laetitiam salutaris tui, et spiritum principali confirma me* ("Restore to me the joy of your salvation, and sustain in me a willing spirit").

5. Ferdinand Ebner (1882–1931) was an elementary school teacher in Gablitz near Vienna and a personal-dialogical philosopher who, together with Martin Buber, is considered one of the most significant dialogical thinkers. His most important work is *The Word and Its Spiritual Realities: Pneumatological Fragments* (1921).

6. *Gröfaz* was a nickname mockingly given to Adolf Hitler after the defeat of the German troops at Stalingrad in 1943. It is the abbreviation of the (ironic) German words for "greatest commander of all time," *größter Feldherr aller Zeiten*.

7. Reinhold Schneider (1903–58) was a German writer. His last book was *Winter in Vienna* (1957/58).

8. Friedrich Heer (1916–83) was a cultural historian, writer, and editor. The most thematically relevant of his many works is perhaps *Der Glaube des Adolf Hitler: Anatomie einer politischen Religiosität* (The Faith of Adolf Hitler: Anatomy of a Political Religiousness) (Vienna, 1968).

9. Adolf Hitler, *My Struggle*, trans. unknown (London: Hurst and Blackett, 1938).

10. Eric Voegelin (1901–85) was a German-American political scientist and philosopher. The fifth volume of his *Collected Works* (St. Louis: University of Missouri Press, 1999) contains *The Political Religions* as well as *The New Science of Politics* and *Science, Politics, and Gnosticism*.

11. *sub specie boni* (Lat.): under the sight of the good, that is, from the point of view of goodness.

12. Vienna's tramline 38 ends at Am Schottenring station (informally known as "JonasReindl") near the University of Vienna.

13. Bruno Brehm (1892–1974), who wrote under the pen name of Bruno Clemens, was an Austrian author. He was a member

of the National Socialist Bamberg Poets' Circle and publisher of the periodical *Der getreue Eckart* from 1938 to 1942.

14. In "Mankind" (*Menschheit*, trans. James Reidel, *Mudlark* 53 [2014]), Austrian poet Georg Trakl (1887–1914) writes,

Mankind marched up before fiery jaws,
A drumroll, the gloomy soldiers' foreheads,
Footsteps through a bloody fog; black iron rings,
Desperation, night in sorrowful minds:
Here Eve's shadow, a manhunt and red coin.

Clouds, the light is breaking through, the Last Supper.
A gentle silence dwells in bread and wine.
And those gathered here are twelve in number.
Nights they moan asleep beneath olive boughs;
Saint Thomas dips his hand in the wound's mark.

15. Ernst Wiechert (1887–1950) was among the most widely read German writers of the "Inner Emigration" under National Socialism.

16. Georg Thurmair (1909–84) was a German writer, poet, journalist, and documentary filmmaker. He authored approximately three hundred German-language hymns.

17. Theodor Innitzer (1875–1955) was the archbishop of Vienna, as well as a professor of New Testament studies and sometime social minister under Engelbert Dollfuß's Austrofascist government.

3. DECISION

1. Father Heinrich Maier (1908–45) was an Austrian Roman Catholic priest, pedagogue, and philosopher. He fought in the resistance against Hitler.

2. 1 Kgs 3:16–28: "Later, two women who were prostitutes came to the king and stood before him. The one woman said, 'Please, my lord, this woman and I live in the same house; and I gave birth while she was in the house. Then on the third day after I gave birth, this woman also gave birth. We were together; there was no one else with us in the house, only the two of us were in the house. Then this woman's son died in the night, because she lay on him. She got up in the middle of the night and took my son from beside me while your servant slept. She laid him at her breast, and laid her dead son at my breast. When I rose in the morning to nurse my son, I saw that he was dead; but when I looked at him closely in the morning, clearly it was not the son I had borne.' But the other woman said, 'No, the living son is mine, and the dead son is yours.' The first said, 'No, the dead son is yours, and the living son is mine.' So they argued before the king.

Then the king said, 'The one says, "This is my son that is alive, and your son is dead"; while the other says, "Not so! Your son is dead, and my son is the living one."' So the king said, 'Bring me a sword,' and they brought a sword before the king. The king said, 'Divide the living boy in two; then give half to the one, and half to the other.' But the woman whose son was alive said to the king—because compassion for her son burned within her—'Please, my lord, give her the living boy; certainly do not kill him!' The other said, 'It shall be neither mine nor yours; divide it.' Then the king responded: 'Give the first woman the living boy; do not kill him. She is his mother.' All Israel heard of the judgment that the king had rendered; and they stood in awe of the king, because they perceived that the wisdom of God was in him, to execute justice."

3. *Der goldene Wagen* (*The Golden Wagon*) (1947–49). The first issue of the first volume was published Easter 1947. Characterized by attractive design and pictures, the periodical continued to appear monthly, in DIN A4 format, until the third volume, which was somewhat larger.

4. Sterz refers to a way of preparing simple dishes with small chunks of buckwheat flour (*Heidensterz*), cornmeal (*Türkensterz*), rye flour (*Brennsterz*), semolina (*Grießsterz*), potatoes (*Erdäpfelsterz*), or beans (*Bohnensterz*). Sterz was a typical "poor people's food," and today, farmers and field workers in Carinthia (*Kärnten*) and Styria (*Steiermark*) still frequently eat Sterz with bacon fat and cracklings as a hearty breakfast.

5. The Monastery community of Mount Saviour was founded in 1950/52 by Fathers Damasus Winzen from Maria Laach, Gregory Bornstedt, and Placid Cormey, the latter two from Portsmouth Priory, Rhode Island.

6. Wilhelm Koppers, SVD (1886–1961), was a German Catholic priest and ethnographer, as well as a Steyler missionary and early member of the "Vienna Kulturkreis School" in cultural anthropology. He was considered a vehement critic and opponent of National Socialist race theory.

7. Wilhelm Schmidt, SVD (1868–1954), was a Roman Catholic priest, linguist, and ethnographer. He founded the "Vienna Kulturkreis School," which attempted to develop a universal history of culture; Schmidt is today considered one of the early twentieth century's most significant comparative linguists.

8. Hubert Rohracher (1903–72) was an Austrian psychologist, philosopher, and jurist. His arguably most famous work, *Persönlichkeit und Schicksal* (Personality and Fate), was published in Vienna in 1926.

9. Walter Schücker, OCist (1913–77), was confessor, counselor, and leader of spiritual exercises at the Cistercian Abbey of Heiligenkreuz. In 1951, he and Abbot Karl Braunstorfer founded the prayer community "Friends of the Holy Cross," which today counts eighteen hundred members. They subsequently founded the Heiligenkreuz Oblate community in 1972.

10. Paul Claudel (1868–1955) was a French writer, poet, and diplomat.

4. BECOMING A MONK

1. German poet Rainer Maria Rilke (1875–1926) writes the following in his *Sonnets to Orpheus* I,7, in *The Poetry of Rilke*, trans. Edward Snow (New York: North Point, 2009), 363:

> Praising, that's it! One appointed to praise he came forth
> like ore out of the stone's silence. His heart, O ephemeral
> winepress for a vintage eternal to man.
>
> Never does his voice die or turn to dust when the divine
> moment seizes him. All becomes vineyard, all becomes
> grape, ripened in his sentient South.
>
> Not mold in the vaults of kings
> nor any shadow falling from the gods
> can give his songs the lie.
>
> He is one of the messengers who stay, holding far into the
> doors of the dead bowls heaped with fruit to be praised.

2. John Henry Newman (1801–90), *The Mission of the Benedictine Order*.

3. See Gen 2:19: "So out of the ground the LORD God formed every animal of the field and every bird of the air, and brought them to the man to see what he would call them; and whatever the man called every living creature, that was its name."

4. The Abbaye SaintPierre de Solesmes is a Benedictine monastery in Solesmes in the French département of Sarthe.

5. Rainer Maria Rilke, *Es winkt zu Fühlung fast aus allen Dingen*, trans. David Young, Cortland Review (Summer 2013).

6. Rainer Maria Rilke, *Sonnets to Orpheus* I,9. in *Duino Elegies & the Sonnets to Orpheus*, trans. Stephen Mitchell (New York: Vintage, 2009), 99.

7. Rainer Maria Rilke, *Duino Elegies*, I, Ninth Elegy, in *Duino Elegies & the Sonnets to Orpheus*, 57.

8. T. S. Eliot, "Burnt Norton," from *Four Quartets, in Collected Poems 1909–1962* (New York: Harcourt Brace & Company, 1991), 180.

9. Raimon Panikkar (1918–2010) was a Roman Catholic priest from Catalonia, Spain. He was a significant proponent of interfaith dialogue and published numerous works on the subject, including *The Trinity and the Religious Experience of Man* and *The Silence of God: The Answer of the Buddha*.

10. Joseph Gredt, OSB (1863–1940), from Luxembourg was a Benedictine monk and philosophy professor in Rome.

11. Evagrius Ponticus (345–99) was an Egyptian monk and theologian who lived in the Nitrian desert with other desert fathers. He originated the "eight patterns of evil," which were then taken up and developed by John Cassian and survive today as the doctrine of the Seven Deadly Sins.

12. The *Apophthegmata Patrum* is a collection of sayings (*apophthegmata*) and stories attributed to the desert fathers of the fourth and fifth centuries AD. The sayings of Abba Poemen, Abba Macarius of Egypt, and Anthony the Great are among the more well known. The *apophthegmata* are similar to the *koans* of Zen Buddhism.

13. Rabbi Samson ben Raphael Hirsch (1808–88) was one of nineteenth-century Germany's leading proponents of Orthodox Judaism and founder of neo-Orthodoxy.

14. Abraham Joshua Heschel (1907–72) was a rabbi, writer, and Jewish religious philosopher of Polish descent. Exiled to the United States, he was active in the civil rights movement. His writing—such as *Man's Quest for God* (New York: Scribner, 1954)—and engagement were officially honored by Pope Paul VI, among others.

15. Rainer Maria Rilke, "Archaic Torso of Apollo," in *The Poetry of Rilke*, ed. and trans. Edward Snow (New York: North Point Press, 2009), 223.

16. Friedrich Nietzsche, *Beyond Good and Evil: Prelude to a Philosophy of the Future*, trans. Judith Norman., ed. Judith Norman and Peter Horstmann (Cambridge: Cambridge University Press, 2002), 4.

17. Friedrich Nietzsche, *The Gay Science: With a Prelude in Rhymes and an Appendix of Songs*, trans. Walter Kaufmann (New York: Vintage Books, 1974), 181.

18. Negative theology attempts to marry religious faith with the philosophy of reason and to explain religious faith using philosophical tools. It denies the possibility of objective knowledge or proof of God. Characteristics, names, or definitions of the Divine are likewise dismissed as insufficient to describe the distinction of the Divine Mystery. One of negative theology's most well-known proponents is the medieval theologian and philosopher Meister Eckhart.

5. INTERFAITH ENCOUNTERS

1. Gustav Mensching (1901–78) was a scholar of comparative religion whose academic contributions play an important role in interfaith dialogue even today. Mensching was partly responsible for the separation of religious studies from theology and the establishment of the former as an independent discipline of inquiry. Mensching saw religion as "the experiential encounter with the Holy, and responsive action by persons motivated by the Holy" (Stuttgart: Curt E. Schwab, 1959, 18–19; excerpt translated by Peter Dahm Robertson).

2. Thich Nhat Hanh (born 1926) is a Vietnamese Buddhist monk, poet, author, and founder of study centers.

3. David Steindl-Rast, *Deeper Than Words: Living the Apostles' Creed* (New York: Doubleday Religion, 2010).

4. The Global Ethic is the formulation of a fundamental stock of ethical norms and values that can be derived from

religious, cultural, and even philosophical traditions throughout human history. The "Global Ethics Project" is an attempt to describe similarities of the world's religions and to develop out of these fundamental norms a shared Ethic, a brief set of rules that can be accepted by all. The project was initiated by theologian Hans Küng.

5. Gustav Mensching refers to this Mystery as "the Holy," and Rudolf Otto has shown that when we encounter the Holy, we are fascinated and thrilled—that is to say, reverent.

6. *Stabilitas loci* (Latin for "fixedness of place") refers to a nun's or monk's connection to a specific monastery.

7. This second line of the Lutheran hymn "*O Lamm Gottes unschuldig*" (O Lamb of God so blameless), well known throughout German churches, translates to "You have borne all sin / Else we would have to despair."

8. Joseph von Eichendorff (1788–1857) was one of German Romanticism's most significant poets and lyricists. The quoted poem is an excerpt from "*Der Umkehrende*" (Turning Back), translated by Peter Dahm Robertson.

6. HERMIT'S LIFE

1. In the style of *Theophane the Monk*, in *Tales of a Magic Monastery* (New York: The Crossroad Publishing Company, 1981).

2. Rainer Maria Rilke, *The Selected Poetry of Rainer Maria Rilke*, trans. Stephen Mitchel (New York: Vintage Books, 1982), 143.

3. Bear Island lies off the coast of Maine and is one of the five Cranberry Isles.

4. Rilke, *Sonnets to Orpheus*, II,23, in *Duino Elegies & the Sonnets to Orpheus*, trans. Stephen Mitchell (New York: Vintage, 2009).

5. Kathleen Jessie Raine, CBE, (1908–2003) was a British poet, academic, and literary critic. Her writing focused particularly on the works of William Blake, W. B. Yeats, and Thomas Taylor. Founder of the Temenos Academy, she was also highly interested in all forms of spirituality.

6. "Alone with the Alone," or with the All-One. It is one of my favorite phrases used by John Henry Cardinal Newman, referring to his relationship with God as a face-to-face encounter that none should come between. As a young and lonely man at Oriel College, he was once greeted on a solitary stroll by Edward Copleston, who, with a gentlemanly bow, said, "*Numquam minus solus quam cum solus!*" (Never less alone than when alone!). Solitude, many saints have learned, is where one best finds God, and solitude cannot be had without silence.

7. Mary Oliver, "The Summer Day," from *New and Selected Poems* (Boston, MA: Beacon Press, 1992).

8. *Scetis* refers to the Wadi El Natrun, a desert valley in Egypt. The name Scetis comes from the Ancient Egyptian *Sekhet-hemat*, meaning "salt field." The Wadi remains a site of hermitages and monasteries.

9. Henry David Thoreau (1817–62) was an American philosopher and author. He is best known for his book *Walden; Or, Life in the Woods* and his essay "Civil Disobedience."

7. ENCOUNTERS IN TRAVEL

1. The *Kohte* was a type of tent that originated in (autonomous) German youth movements. It was developed around 1930 by Eberhard Koebel, based on a tent design of the Finnish Saami people (near Inari Lake).

2. The *Puszta* is the large steppe region leading from eastern Austria and Hungary all the way to Mongolia. It is probable that Austrian youth movements encountered these kinds of

long-handled spoons on visits to this region, as trips to Hungary, Romania, and other parts of Eastern Europe were popular.

3. Cardinal Pio Taofinu'u, SM (1923–2006), was the archbishop of Samoa-Apia.

4. For the definition and description of a *marae*, see https://en.wikipedia.org/wiki/Marae.

5. The meaning of *Puja* approximates to "honoring" or "doing honor." As a ritual, which should ideally be practiced daily, it is one of the primary parts of everyday religious practice in both Hinduism and Buddhism.

6. Bede Griffiths (1906–93) was a British Benedictine monk and one of the twentieth century's best known mystics. From 1968 onward, he led the Shantivanam ashram and monastery. He is particularly known for his religious dialogue with Hinduism.

7. Rainer Maria Rilke, *Rilke's Book of Hours: Love Poems to God*, trans. Anita Barrows and Joanna Macy (New York: Riverhead Books, 1996), 84.

8. CONTEMPLATION AND REVOLUTION

1. *Sangha* is the community of lay faithful and ordained clergy who mutually support one another in following the Buddha and the Dharma. Regardless of the exact definition, all traditions view *sangha* as one of the Buddhism's "Three Jewels" or "Three Treasures."

2. See http://www.gratefulness.org, http://viviragradecidos.org, and others.

3. Dorothy Day (1897–1980) was an American Christian Socialist and journalist. Until 1927, she was a radical communist; after her conversion to Catholicism in 1928, she advocated a Christian anarchism. Together with Peter Maurin, she founded the Catholic Worker Movement and was imprisoned several times

because, as both a committed suffragist and pacifist, she could not reconcile her conscience and faith to contemporary political developments. In 2000, Pope John Paul II granted the New York Archdiocese permission to open her cause for canonization.

4. Friedrich Hölderlin (1770–1843), from *An Zimmern*; excerpt translated by author.

5. T. S. Eliot, "Burnt Norton," from *Four Quartets, in Collected Poems 1909–1962* (New York: Harcourt Brace & Company, 1991), 176.

6. See www.gratefulness.org.

9. DOUBLE REALM

1. Rainer Maria Rilke, *Sonnets to Orpheus* I,9, in *The Poetry of Rilke*, trans. Edward Snow (New York: North Point, 2009), 367.

2. T. S. Eliot, "Little Gidding," from *Four Quartets*, in *Collected Poems 1909–1962* (New York: Harcourt Brace & Company, 1991), 204.

3. Rainer Maria Rilke, *Rilke's Book of Hours: Love Poems to God*, trans. Anita Barrows and Joanna Macy (New York: Riverhead Books, 1996), 69.

4. Dupuytren's contracture is a thickening and shortening of the connective tissues (fascia) of the palm, most commonly observed around Haithabu, the Viking capital.

5. From the poem "Es ist doch alles nur aus Liebe gut" by German poet and literary critic Will Vesper (1882–1962). Excerpt translated by Peter Dahm Robertson.

6. T. S. Eliot, "The Dry Salvages," from *Four Quartets* in *Collected Poems 1909–1962*, 199.

7. Rainer Maria Rilke: "Nous sommes les abeilles de l'Univers. Nous butinons éperdument le miel du visible, pour l'accumuler dans la grande ruche d'or de l'Invisible." Letter to W. von Hulewicz.

8. W. B. Yeats, *Sailing to Byzantium*, accessed July 7, 2017, https://www.poets.org/poetsorg/poem/sailing-byzantium.

9. P. Otto Mauer, summarizing Thornton Wilder's novel *The Bridge of San Luis Rey*.

10. *Sonnets to Orpheus* I, 9.

11. Clive Staples Lewis (1898–1963) was an Irish writer and literary scholar. In addition to his scholarship and criticism, he also published many works of Christian apologia (e.g., *Mere Christianity* and *The Abolition of Man*) and novels such as *The Great Divorce* and *The Chronicles of Narnia*.

12. Cappadocia is a region in Asia Minor. In the fourth century AD, it was home to many significant figures in early Christianity. Three of these—Basil the Great, Gregory of Nyssa, and Gregory of Nazianzus—are today known as the Cappadocian Fathers. They were early advocates of a trinitarian theory of God as God the Father, God the Son, and God the Holy Spirit.

13. Rainer Maria Rilke, "Letter to Witold von Hulewicz, November 13, 1925" in *Duino Elegies*, trans. Edward Snow (New York: North Point, 2009), 70.

14. The definition is taken from Thomas Aquinas.

15. Edward Estlin Cummings (1894–1962) was an American poet and writer, generally known as e.e. cummings.

16. "Extinguish My Eyes, I'll Go on Seeing You." Rainer Maria Rilke, *Rilke's Book of Hours: Love Poems to God*, 111–12.

17. "Only in Our Doing Can We Grasp You," from Rainer Maria Rilke, *Rilke's Book of Hours: Love Poems to God*, 84; last two lines appended to incomplete translation.

ABOUT THE INTERVIEWER

Johannes Kaup studied philosophy and Catholic theology at the University of Vienna and is a trained psychotherapist in Daseins-analysis. He has been active in the field of youth social work and as a religious lecturer. Since 1990, he has been working at ORF, the Austrian Broadcasting Corporation, where he has conceived and moderated programs in religion, science, and education.

He has received numerous awards as a journalist, among others with the "Radiopreis de Erwachsenenbildung," the "Austrian Climate Protection Prize," the "Seniors' Rose," and the "Dr. Karl Renner Prize for Literature" in the Radio category.

Johannes Kaup has been a moderator at international congresses and has published five books.